A Life Outdoors

To the Russell + District Regional Library

[signature]
Aug 7, 2015

DATE DUE										Cat. No. 23-221
SEP 2 5 2015										
JAN 0 2 2016										BRODART, CO.

"I went to the woods because I wished to live deliberately, to front only the essential facts of life, and see if I could not learn what it had to teach, and not, when I came to die, discover that I had not lived."

Henry David Thoreau
Walden; or, Life in the Woods

RUSSELL AND DISTRICT REGIONAL LIBRARY

3 6730 00013083 1

 **FriesenPress**

Suite 300 – 852 Fort Street
Victoria, BC, Canada V8W 1H8
www.friesenpress.com

Copyright © 2014 by Robert D. Sopuck
First Edition — 2014

Foreward by Monte Hummel.

All rights reserved.

No part of this publication may be reproduced in any form, or by any means, electronic or mechanical, including photocopying, recording, or any information browsing, storage, or retrieval system, without permission in writing from the publisher.

ISBN
978-1-4602-4526-2 (Hardcover)
978-1-4602-4527-9 (Paperback)
978-1-4602-4528-6 (eBook)

1. Sports & Recreation, Hunting

Distributed to the trade by The Ingram Book Company

Table of Contents

Foreword xi

Preface xiii

Introduction 1

Why We Hunt 4

Where Do We Draw the Line? 7

Reflections from the Deer Stand 10

Keeping the
Memories and Traditions Alive 13

A Reader's Letter 15

The Charm of Fly Fishing 18

In Praise of Poplar 22

Manitoba Deer
Season Provides Many Lessons 25

Spring Hunting Opportunities Abound ... 28

Signs of Spring, or You Are What You Eat ... 32

Late October: a Time of Transition ... 34

Stories in the Snow ... 37

Hunting Reflections ... 40

Unique Wildlife Experiences a Part of Country Living ... 43

A Manitoba Artisan ... 46

A Man for All Seasons ... 50

A Manitoba Conservation Pioneer ... 53

A Passion for Waterfowling ... 56

My Favourite Country Store ... 59

A Call to a Neighbour ... 62

On Having a Hunting Dog ... 65

On Choosing a Deer Rifle ... 68

Sighting In Your Big Game Rifle ... 71

A Late Season Upland Bird Hunt ... 73

A Hunting Day to Remember ... 77

A Wild Turkey at Last ... 80

Lessons Learned on the Hunting Trails ... 84

Your Eyes in the Woods ... 86

Hunting Whitetails in the Big Woods of the Boreal Forest ... 89

Today the Elk Won ... 92

Paralyzed by Elk ... 94

The White-Tailed Deer's Fall Drama ... 96

The Ruffed Grouse—A Manitoba Treasure ... 99

Being in the Woods Has Its Own Rewards ... 102

Nature in Action ... 104

Rattling for Big Bucks Works for Veteran Hunter ... 106

The Joys of Late Season Ruffed Grouse Hunting ... 108

Try Hunting Teal This Year ... 112

Big Game Hunting Much More Affordable than You Think ... 115

Trapping and the Fur Trade: Canada's Oldest Industry ... 117

Manitoba Beavers: The Good, the Bad, and the Ugly ... 119

Mother and Daughter Preserve Family's Hunting Tradition ... 123

Stacy Gets Her First Moose ... 126

Buying and Trying that First Shotgun ... 129

First Deer Stories ... 132

The Rewards of Being a Youth Hunt Mentor ... 136

The Family that Hunts Together......139

The North American Model of Wildlife Management......141

The Paradox of Hunting......143

The Man who Changed the Face of Conservation......145

Surviving a Tough Winter......147

Waterfowl Hunters' Gift to Mother Nature......150

Hardy Transplant Thriving in Manitoba......153

Eat Beef If You Care About Environmental Conservation......156

Food for Thought......159

Do-It-Yourself Venison Steaks and Roasts......162

Preparing Wild Game for the Table......165

Cooking Wild Game Birds......171

Morel Mushrooms and Fiddlehead Ferns: Two Spring Treats......175

Wild Berries Add a Wonderful Dimension to Rural Life......178

Putting Food By......181

Wild Spring Foods Create Delightful Meals......185

Preparing Early Season Geese for the Table......187

Wine and Wild Game......190

The Inestimable Caroline......193

The Gift 196

A Granddaughter Comes into Our Lives 198

Hunting with Dad 201

This Has Been a Wonderful Journey 205

Afterword 207

About the Author 208

Foreword

As someone who was raised in the bush in northwestern Ontario, I often find myself advising my urban colleagues on how things they propose to say or do will go over in the northern, rural and coastal parts of our country. Our habit of generating conservation plans, in large cities, that need to be actually implemented elsewhere, can lead to big trouble if we're not careful.

So… along comes my old friend Bob Sopuck, with a book title—every word of which invites trouble, or at least risks being out of sync with the times: First, "a life outdoors," when sitting under artificial lighting at a keyboard has become the norm. Second, "essays on hunting and gathering," when shopping is how most Canadians get all their food. And third, "country living in the 21st century," when eighty percent of Canadians live in urban environments.

Does this make Bob's book just a throwback to earlier times? I don't think so. I take it more as a reminder, for the present and the future, that a significant number of us will continue to live rewarding lives outside the city. In fact, we couldn't live life any other way.

Okay, but does his book inflame our differences? After all, Bob's unashamed Conservative credentials can be provocative, and he does have opinions. Well, I for one have never believed that any single political party has cornered the market when it comes to being concerned about the environment. We should expect the best from all of them. For example, during WWF's ten-year Endangered Spaces Campaign, the greatest gains were made by the "two Mikes"—NDP Premier Mike Harcourt in BC and Conservative Premier Mike Harris in Ontario, and we received strong support from Manitoba's Gary Filmon, when both Bob and his wife Caroline served as policy advisors in that government.

The truth is this: There are good people on all sides. The trick is to find them and to work together on mutual concerns. Certainly Bob's deep connection to the traditions and landscape of his homeplace shines through on every page. Fundamentally, we all need to hang onto the underlying ecological processes and habitat that make wildlife possible in the first place—whether you're motivated to capture it with a paintbrush, a camera, a firearm … or a book. Otherwise, we risk fiddling while Rome burns. And no matter what your motivation, shared experiences such as a sunrise over a marsh should bring us together—not drive us apart.

The revered conservationist (and hunter) Aldo Leopold described such a sunrise as a time "when you hear a mallard being audibly enthusiastic about his soup" and "when a block of bluebills, pitching pondward, tears the dark silk of heaven in one long rending nose-dive." Based on that, I'll let you decide whether a hunter can't also be a poet.

The fact is that Nature has the power to bridge our human differences. And I believe Bob Sopuck has gone to that shared source with this book. So step outdoors with him, to breathe, touch, taste and conserve something that inspires—and ultimately sustains—us all.

Monte Hummel
President Emeritus, World Wildlife Fund Canada

Preface

In 2001, I was provided with an opportunity to write the hunting column for the *Winnipeg Free Press*, Manitoba's largest daily circulation newspaper. Up to that time, I had been advocating for hunting, angling, trapping, and the rural way of life as a staff person for the Delta Waterfowl Foundation. So the chance to speak to a largely urban audience about my passion for my way of life simply could not be passed up. My column, which ran for eight years, was about the "lifestyle of a hunter" as opposed to a column about "how to hunt." As I noted in my final column, there are many more expert hunters than I, but to me, I thought that my way of life in the country, alongside my wife, the inestimable Caroline, might be of interest to others. We live in a log house on 480 acres of land in the country south of Riding Mountain National Park in Manitoba. We are essentially self-sufficient in terms of food, we heat with wood and do our best to conserve and improve that slice of heaven we call "The Farm."

Hunting, angling, fish and wildlife are an integral part of what we do and who we are. Eating wild food is a kind of communion for us; constantly reminding us about our connections with the natural world.

This book is a compendium of some of my columns with a number of new ones that had not been previously published. With this book, dear reader, Caroline and I hope to share with you our passion for the hunter's life, country living, the natural world and our place within it.

A Life Outdoors

Essays on Hunting, Gathering and Country Living in the 21st Century

Robert D. Sopuck

Introduction

(It All Started with This Fish)

My life outdoors can be traced to a couple of tiny family cottages on the shores of Dorothy Lake, which is a widening of the Winnipeg River in eastern Manitoba. On this particular summer day in 1955, my dad, mom, and a number of uncles and aunts were working on cottage projects, but being only four, I was spared the requirement to work. But ever the eager beaver, I begged to be able to "help", so Dad, very wisely as it turned out, asked me if I wanted to fish instead.

"Sure!" I exclaimed. And maybe that was my plan all along.

So Dad rigged up an old steel fishing pole with no reel but a stout four-foot piece of line tied to the end of the pole. And to the end of the line he affixed an old favourite, the red and white Dardevle. Then it was back to work for him, but I was fishing! So I started flinging that old Dardevle into the water and then pulling it for a couple of feet causing it to spin once or twice underwater before I whipped it back into the air and thence back into the water. Now that I think about it, it was a primitive kind of fly-fishing, and I'm damn lucky I didn't embed the hooks in the back of my head!

I had been at it for ten minutes or so when the unthinkable happened; a four-pound northern pike, or jackfish as we called them back then, grabbed that old Dardevle and tried to drag it, with me attached, back to deeper water. I don't recall exactly what happened, but I dug the butt of that rod into my stomach and hung on for dear life. It was me against the fish in a kind of "Young Man and the Sea" saga, but I was grimly determined to not let that fish get away. Pretty quickly I realized that I needed help, so I started yelling at the top of my voice. Obviously the adults presumed the worst, so they all came running. Dad quickly sized up the situation and ran up to me, grabbed the line, and hauled that old northern pike up on the rocks. I started to shake with excitement, and everyone was yelling stuff like, "way to go, Robert," "what a big jackfish," "you got a nice fish!" A number of pictures were taken, and through it all, my dad was beaming. This is a human story that has played itself out for hundreds and thousands of years. A young hunter, his first kill, with his father present, and embraced by an entire family.

Robert and his Dad with That First Fish, circa 1955

Since that fish, I have had careers in fisheries biology, natural resources management, agriculture, wildlife conservation, forestry, and outdoor writing. In my twenties I moved to the country where my wife Caroline and I are the stewards of 480 of the most beautiful acres on God's green Earth. And I'm a member of the Canadian Parliament as well. Through it all, the memory of that fish, and perhaps its spirit too, has always been with me. Maybe that is why I am such a passionate conservationist; I want to have as many kids as possible experience what I have.

I don't recall what happened to that fish—I presume he became supper—but that first fish burned into me a desire to be outdoors, to conserve Nature, to hunt, and to fish with a passion that has yet to diminish. Dad and Mom have sadly passed on, but what they gave to me will live forever. This book is dedicated to Joseph and Ida Sopuck.

Why We Hunt

(May 2007)

"Why do you hunt?" It is a question all hunters have been asked. You are at a loss for words after you've given all of the usual answers relating to tradition, economics, wildlife management, and food. Your questioner has challenged all of your points and, as far as your "hunting is a tradition" argument, dismisses it by saying, "Slavery was a tradition too and we got rid of that." Now what?

The "rational" reasons to hunt are strangely inadequate. We must go beyond these admittedly valid utilitarian aspects of hunting into the realms of spirituality and philosophy for deep answers to deep questions.

Hunters have their very own philosopher, José Ortega y Gasset, who wrote *Meditations on Hunting* in 1942. Gasset asks, "Consequently, aware that it is a more difficult matter than it seems at first, I ask myself, what the devil kind of occupation is hunting?" He explores in minute detail the "occupation of hunting," in chapters titled "Hunting and Happiness" and "The Essence of Hunting," among others.

In describing hunting's spiritual nature, Gasset says, "Strictly speaking, the essence of sportive hunting is not raising the animal to the level of man, but something much more spiritual than that: a conscious and almost religious humbling of man which limits his superiority and lowers him towards the animal." Thus we have the rules, norms and ethics of hunting that ensure a "fair chase" and sustainable populations. In my case, I won't shoot a ruffed grouse on the ground, but only flying. Some hunters refuse to shoot female deer whereas I don't have any compunction about taking a doe. And so it goes.

The killing of an animal is the natural end of the hunt and definitely the goal of hunting itself, *but not necessarily the goal of the hunter*. Being given a dead deer is much different than hunting it for oneself. Gasset says of hunting, "the tactile drama of its actual capture, and usually even more the tragedy of its death, nurture the hunter's interest through anticipation and give liveliness and authenticity to all the previous work." Now we are getting somewhere with his use of the word *authenticity*.

Authenticity refers to something that is genuine, pure, uncorrupted and in the best sense of the word "real." Hunting is an authentic experience simply because it is so real. And its authenticity that seems so lacking in the modern world.

The University of Alberta's Lee Foote is a scientist, writer and hunter. Foote compares hunting to other modern human activities like video games, sports, and TV that substitute for reality. In his article "The Irreducibility of Hunting," he says, "Hunting moves us from the vicarious to reality. We hunt not only to take life but to give authenticity to our lives." Hunting is one of the few truly authentic experiences open to modern people.

The taking of life bothers many people, especially those who are a generation or two removed from the farm. Foote reminds us that, "In the long pageantry of anticipation, preparation, practice, apprenticeship, travel, pursuit, killing, possessing, processing, sharing, consuming, telling, re-telling, analyzing, speculating, and appreciating, the actual kill is one step on a long winding staircase." He further notes that "Hunting without the intent to kill is not hunting in the same way that dress rehearsal is not theatre."

The storytelling tradition goes back a thousand generations; right back to paleolithic man. Just imagine that hunting group huddled by torchlight in a cave in what is now Europe. They tell and re-tell great hunting stories that ultimately end up as humanity's first great works of art; hunting scenes painted on rocks. Maybe the purpose of hunting is to get stories? The meat is soon consumed, but the stories live on. Live on and on to inspire new generations of hunters.

Dr. Randall Eaton, an evolutionary psychologist has written a book entitled *From Boys to Men of Heart—Hunting as a Rite of Passage* and argues that "wildlife management in general has failed terribly to grasp the psycho-spiritual dimensions [of hunting] as its social relevance to the development of youth." According to Eaton, only hunting connects men profoundly to nature. He says, "The instinct to hunt awakens spontaneously in boys, but the taking of life opens the heart and tempers that instinct with compassion. If we want to transform boys into men who respect life and are responsible to society and the environment, we need to mentor them in hunting as a rite of passage." He goes on to say, "The hunt is the ideal way to teach universal values, including generosity, patience, courage, fortitude and humility."

As Lee Foote writes: "The hunt is primal, timeless, elemental and irreducible. Hunting continues to renew us, give us humbling mortality insights, and providing hope. There are so very few things in our lives that yield these most precious of gifts; renewal, humility, insight, and hope. We must treat hunting with the same reverence we hold for our religions, our children, and the world's greatest works of art."

What these philosophers are telling us is that hunting makes us human.

A Day Afield

Where Do We Draw the Line?

(January 2004)

Some recent events moved me to think about ethics; more specifically the ethics of hunting and our relationships to animals.

Firstly, I was asked to provide a commentary on the popular morning talk show *Adler-on-Line*. The issue was about a wounded deer with an arrow in its side that appeared at a backyard in the Bird's Hill area. The homeowner was outraged and sent an impassioned email to Charles Adler questioning why this happened and, by extension, questioning the ethics of all hunters.

Secondly, again on Adler, a voicemail recording was broadcast in which an obviously distraught woman described, according to the story she saw in the snow, the running down of a jackrabbit by a snowmobile.

We have become very sensitized to these kinds of issues. Regarding animals, some question the ethics of hunting, often in the context of modern hunting being "unfair" to the animal.

The ethical dimensions of hunting have been the subject of books, articles, essays, and speeches, and like all human questions, definitive answers are elusive.

Let's take the concept of "fair chase." In hunting terms, it means ensuring that the animal has a fair chance of escaping, whatever *fair* might mean. The reason that the snowmobile story disgusts all but the most immoral among us is that it was so clearly unfair. The jackrabbit is superbly adapted to life on the open plains, but snowmobiles are not part of that equation (for the record, I am a snowmobile owner). The jackrabbit is a most worthy quarry for the hunter on foot, and successful jackrabbit hunts are rare. Yet we recoil at the cruelty of running a jackrabbit down by machine even though the results of hunting on foot or chasing it by machine can be exactly the same; a dead jackrabbit. We have made an ethical distinction.

Now this was an easy case, but what happens when it's not so clear cut. Take the archery deer example above. The outraged homeowner suggested that using a firearm would have been more humane (and hence ethical) because the animal would have been killed cleanly. But bow hunting has increased in popularity precisely because of the challenges it presents. Shooting a deer with a rifle at 100 metres is not difficult, but all that a bow hunter can do with a deer at that range is wave goodbye. Does that make bow hunting more *fair*? Maybe for some, since the percentage of bow hunters who take deer is but a small fraction of the success rate of rifle hunters.

The ethical dilemmas get even stickier when we compare our hunting practices with other hunters and make the decision that what "we" do is morally superior to what "they" do. The great conservationist Aldo Leopold, in his 1949 book *A Sand County Almanac*, deplored the ever-increasing improvement in technology which demeaned the outdoor experience, at least for him. My hunting clothes use the most modern fabrics, and I have a modern rifle with a 'scope (some think this unfair), but I cannot bring myself to use electronics when I hunt. For others, a GPS has become an indispensable piece of equipment, and who is to say they are wrong. Certainly not me. I will only take a ruffed grouse that is flying, while others will take them on the ground knowing how good the bird tastes. I will shoot a doe deer, while others take male deer only, arguing that my taking of a female is immoral.

And in terms of technology, when does it become too much? The great Spanish philosopher Ortega y Gasset in his book *Meditations on Hunting* stressed that the essence of sportive hunting requires "a conscious and almost religious humbling of man which limits his superiority and lowers him towards the animal." Too much technology and it's really not a hunt any more, is it? But where we draw the line must, of necessity, be a personal decision, and we must be very careful about issuing moral judgments about the practices of others for the tables could soon be turned back on us.

Thus the development of a hunter's moral code is a personal process. What may have been acceptable in your youth is abandoned as you get older, even as you have obeyed every hunting law on the books. Personal ethical codes change, but as we age, the tendency for most of us is to limit our technical superiority over the animal for the simple reason, among others, that we want to extend the hunting process as long as we can.

Lastly, there are no rewards, or penalties for that matter, for what we do on the hunt. Aldo Leopold noted, "A peculiar virtue of wildlife ethics is that the hunter ordinarily has no gallery to applaud or disapprove of his conduct. Whatever his acts, they are dictated by his own conscience…" Here is the answer then: Let your conscience be your guide.

Reflections from the Deer Stand

(November 2008)

I am somewhat of a bumbling white-tailed deer hunter in that I rely as much on luck as opposed to skill to get my venison in the freezer. I'm not a bad deer hunter, but my deer hunting skills pale in comparison with some of the more expert deer stalkers who work at it over the entire year.

Don't get me wrong, I love deer hunting, and Caroline and I have never yet had a winter without venison in our freezer. Nevertheless, I approach deer hunting in a somewhat dreamy state of mind, a state that is very conducive to the way I hunt, which is to tuck myself into a nice little clump of bush beside a deer trail and then wait—and hope—for a deer to walk by. I've taken many deer with this technique. It's usually a very easy shot that results in a clean kill. One shot and *voilà!* Venison for the winter.

One would think that sitting still for hours on end would be quite boring, but for many of us it's time well spent. In fact, you find out that time both passes very quickly but very slowly. You are in a relaxed but alert "trance," not unlike meditation. You notice every bird, every movement, and every sound. Every crunched leaf makes you think, *deer are coming*. But most of the time it's either a squirrel or a ruffed grouse out foraging on the forest floor. And speaking of ruffed grouse, many is the time when I've been startled by a "ruffie" flying into a nearby poplar tree for its evening feed of tender buds.

CURIOUS DOE APPROACHES DEER STAND

Sitting on the deer stand often gets me thinking about what marvellous animals white-tailed deer are. They look fragile and delicate but are as tough as nails when it comes to surviving in what can be a very harsh world. Everybody wants to eat them, Manitoba winters can be brutal, and sometimes food can be hard to find. White-tails can be real fighters when they have to. I once witnessed a year-old deer fight off a hungry coyote by charging directly at the predator, stomping its feet all the while snorting like a prize fighter. The coyote slunk off, knowing that this young deer was not quite the easy meal he had anticipated.

The physiology of a white-tailed deer also contributes to its survival. One biologist described deer as animals whose bloodstream resembles a "working hospital" that greatly speeds up the clotting process should the animal be injured. Many a hunter has marvelled at the stamina of a deer and that's due to the animal's unique physiology. During especially cold spells in winter, deer will cease feeding and bed down, conserving energy until the next warm spell; a kind of "hibernation" if you will. Somehow they know that the act of feeding would take more energy than the food itself would produce.

White-tails in the northern part of their range have big, *rounded* bodies, the better to conserve heat, while their southern cousins are small and *angular*, the better to dissipate heat. It is for these reasons that white-tails thrive from Alaska to Central America.

Keeping the Memories and Traditions Alive

(August 2010)

December 4, 2002. "Hunted grouse at home. Molly and I hunted north of the house and flushed 5 beautiful ruffed grouse. Pretty wary birds but we managed to follow one up and collect it with the side-by-side 20 gauge. Nice retrieve. Big male with aspen buds, rose hips, and snowberries in his crop."

I closed my hunting journal and reflected on that particular day; one of my very last hunts with Molly, my old Chesapeake Bay Retriever. She died a while ago, and even though I've got a dandy replacement in my big male Chesapeake, Mountie, I can always relive my hunts with her in the pages of my hunting journal.

Journals are like photo albums; kind of a pain to work on at first but ultimately worth it. And as the years go by, words and pictures of past adventures become real treasures. It could be my age or the time of year (the glorious fall is almost upon us!), but I'm going back over my journals these days with increasing frequency. Maybe it's merely a futile effort to stop time, but days afield are so precious that I never want to let them go.

All hunters and anglers should think about keeping a journal. Not only will a journal keep outdoor memories alive, it soon becomes a valuable database that you can access to give you guidance about planning future hunts. And as an added bonus, a journal is a great way to deal with disputes with hunting partners who insist they shot better on a hunt than they really did. Your journal can settle those arguments once and for all!

An even more important reason to start and keep an outdoor journal is when your children (or in my case, grandchild!) start to hunt and fish with you. You will undoubtedly take lots of pictures of the child's first fish or grouse, but the written word simply cannot be replaced. An added bonus is that you will be able to chart the progress of the youngster as they progress in the field and be able to relive the memories over and over with them. And with the new desktop publishing programs one can combine the journal entries with photographs and create a lasting record of those great days in the field.

Starting a journal is like planting a tree. An old forester was once asked when the best time was to plant a tree. He replied, "The two best times to plant a tree are fifty years ago and right now." It's the same with a journal. I started my angling journal in 1995 and my hunting journal in 1996 and am now building a real nice record.

And don't think that you need to write an essay about the day's activities. I just jot down a few points about the weather and the hunting spot, a note about the dog work, a bit about the animals' behaviour and feeding patterns, and the game that was or was not taken. Elegant prose it ain't, but it does the job. I would advise any hunter or angler to start a journal. You won't regret it.

A Reader's Letter

(August 2009)

There are many good things about being a columnist, but nothing beats thoughtful letters from readers. It has been my hope all along that my columns would be of interest to non-hunters who might share an appreciation for the way of life that many of us choose to live. Below is one such letter.

Dear Robert,

My husband and I are avid fishermen. But I find myself drawn to your articles in the Winnipeg Free Press. I'm not responding to you about any one in particular. I enjoy the topics of family togetherness, enjoyment of the outdoors, and other subjects of the week. The reason why I am writing? Even I don't know for sure. Let me give you a bit of history.

As far back as I can remember, I was always animal crazy. When I was in my teens, my sister married a wonderful man. He was wonderful until I found out he hunted. I could not understand how anyone can take a life of a living, breathing being. Fast forward a bit to my adult years, and my husband introduced me to fishing. In line with our love for animals, most of our catches are safely returned to the water unharmed. The only ones we keep, are the ones we have damaged and we know will not survive. I hope you have a good laugh when I tell you that we haven't had a fresh fish meal for years. I used to always joke that I could be a good hunter, if we could to catch and release there too. And it isn't just me. My husband says that if we were farmers, we would end up making pets out of the livestock and end up being vegetarians.

A few years back, one of the new guys at work ended up being a hunting nut, and I say that in the most loving way possible. He was a good kid, who enjoyed hunting with his dad and his grandpa. I started lobbying the boss to allow him to take time off work as early as muzzle loading season, and into the early winter too. My boss was not pleased with me, and wondered how on earth an animal loving person could condone killing. I mentioned to him that as long as he enjoys throwing a steak on the grill he shouldn't talk. Something has to die for him to eat.

Which brings me to another thought. While I don't condone the actions or tactics of PETA, the meaning of the acronym of their name does have merit. I would love for all creatures on this planet to have a good life, till the end. Unfortunately we cannot say this to describe how our food ends up in the pretty packaging at the grocery store. They lead a bleak existence and a gruesome end, with terror all around them on the kill floor. Not a pretty thought to say the least.

While I imagine that some game animals suffer the last few moments of their life, especially at the hands of inexperienced hunters, at least they lived well, and die with much less terror than their farmed counterparts.

When I was growing up I would have never thought a hunter could be a good person. Now I know there are wonderful, family loving people out there, who happen to get some of the food on their table in a respectful way. Give me another twenty *years or so, and who knows, I may be one of those women in the latter part of their life, signing up for the Becoming an Outdoorswoman program! Stranger things have happened. Until then, I'll just keep enjoying your columns.*

Anyway. I just thought I would let you know, that there are non-hunters out there, who do respect you and the lifestyle you have.

Sincerely,
A Reader

The Charm of Fly Fishing

(PREVIOUSLY UNPUBLISHED)

Ever since the movie *A River Runs Through It* was released, the popularity of fly fishing has been growing by leaps and bounds. In my own case, I long preceded that movie and have been fly fishing since I was fifteen. Back in those days we pioneering Canadian fly fishermen had to really work at it. All equipment and materials had to be mail-ordered from the States, and what we were able to obtain was far inferior to the equipment we have today.

Fly fishing as we know it originated in rural England where anglers quickly realized that by imitating the insects that trout fed on they could get more fish in the bag. And since most of these insects floated on the water's surface, the imitations had to be weightless. This posed a dilemma since traditional fishing was done by a weighted lure or bait being flung out to the fish with the cast dependant on the weight of the lure or sinker to pull the line out. At first these fly fishing pioneers would tie a line to a long pole, affix an un-weighted fly at the end and touch it on the water. That was fine for fish close to shore, but they had to devise a method to get that un-weighted fly to any reach in the stream. I'm sure one of these fly fishing pioneers had a *eureka* moment and realized that if you weight and cast the line that weightless concoction of fur and feathers would "go along for the ride," reaching much farther than before. And after that, as they say, the rest is history.

ROBERT FIGHTING A BIG RAINBOW TROUT ON A FLY ROD

For me, fly fishing is an endless journey of discovery, improvisation, invention, natural history, and new lakes and rivers. Whereas, back in the *old days*, trout were considered the only respectable fly fishing quarry, modern fly fishermen have pioneered methods and techniques to catch all manner of species from carp, to bass, to pike, and whitefish and many more. Furthermore, it used to be that fly fishing was considered a sport for shallow waters in streams and rivers, but today's "feather chuckers" have access to fast sinking lines and weighted flies so fly fishing at depths of five to ten metres or more is common. Fly fishermen engage in endless debates about the best fly to use on a certain day, the finest species of fish to pursue, and the merits of various types of fly rods. Actually, if you get three fly casters in a room, you are sure to have four opinions on every fly fishing topic imaginable. Fortunately these are innocent and charming debates with little if any implications for the *outside world*. Or as legendary fly fishermen Bryan Clark and John Goddard point out, "The literature of fly-fishing is a minefield of disagreement on issues of momentous inconsequence."

The beauty of a well-thrown fly cast adds an aesthetic dimension to fly fishing. In fact, there are a number of YouTube videos where fly casting is set to music and the results are quite mind-blowing. And then there are the *flies* themselves; or what are tied to the business end of a fly rod. Actually the term "flies" is a misnomer and a holdover from the days when insect imitations were created to exactly match what a stream trout was feeding on. A skilled fly tier can create imitations that mimic all species of minnows and forage fish, shrimp, crayfish, frogs, mice, and even ducklings! And these creations range in size from two or so millimetres across to monstrosities that can be ten to fifteen centimetres in length. In fact, a good fly tier is limited only by his or her imagination.

Many fly patterns are hundreds of years old, and tiers hew faithfully to the original, and very beautiful, English chalk stream designs. Old patterns like the Royal Coachman (named after the Queen Victoria's coachman who presumably invented the fly) are still in use while the traditional Atlantic salmon flies like the Jock Scott are tied more as works of art. Other and newer patterns have been developed to take advantage of new and emerging fly fishing opportunities. In my own region south of Riding Mountain National Park in Manitoba, aerators have been installed on a number of lakes. Aerators allow the trout to overwinter and take advantage of the incredible natural productivity in these lakes. This development has spawned (pun intended) new fly fishing opportunities, and fly tiers have created new patterns to match what these monster trout feed on. Patterns such as the Psychedelic P-Quad, Phantom-of-the-Lake, Mark's Minnow, Darting Damsel, and Woolly Bugger, among many others, have become "must have" flies in any fly fisherman's arsenal.

Most fly fishermen quickly become fly tiers and spend many pleasant winter months at their benches creating that "just right" fly that will slay the fish come open water. Fly tying is actually quite easy, and once you have mastered the basics, a whole new world opens up. As one wag put it: "If you can tie your shoes you can tie flies." There are uncounted fly patterns to tie or indeed invent, and if you are so inclined, there are numerous blogs and forums where fly tiers endlessly debate the merits of this or that pattern or material. Fly tying dovetails nicely with hunting since the fur and feathers that you bring back from the field can be used to as fly tying material.

I guess if there was one word to describe fly fishing, it would be "charming." One is charmed by the rivers, lakes, fish, the flies, and the art of fly casting itself. The fact that fly fishing is quite frankly of such little significance in the big scheme of things just adds to its charm. We simply do not care about the hours we spend fly casting. Or as noted fly fishing author John Gierach said,

"I used to like fishing because I thought it had some larger significance. Now I like fishing because it is the one thing I can think of that probably doesn't."

May it always be so.

Robert Fly Fishing

In Praise of Poplar

(January 2010)

It's winter and that means it's wood-cutting time in the aspen parklands, and most afternoons will find Caroline and me in the forest bringing out next winter's firewood. Getting your firewood a year ahead of time is standard practice in the country, and most of our neighbours are also spending "quality time" in the "bush." Right now the ground is frozen, and the snow is not too deep, making early winter ideal for wood cutting.

Like most prairie wood burners, we're dependant on aspen since this tree is far and away the most abundant in the entire region; hence the name "aspen parkland." Since we own 320 acres of aspen woods, we have a deep relationship with the tree, but I would not have it any other way. When I use the term aspen, I'm largely referring to the "trembling aspen" or white poplar; the most common aspen species in Manitoba, the other being the balsam poplar or black poplar. According to Gordon Gullion's 1984 book *Managing Northern Forest for Wildlife* (the bible of forest-wildlife management) published by The Ruffed Grouse Society: "The trembling or quaking aspen has the widest distribution of any tree in North America..."

The aspen also happens to have a few interesting traits that make it quite different from your "normal" tree. For one thing aspens are separated into male and female trees whereas most other tree species have flowers of both sexes on the same tree. The male aspen can be distinguished by the very large flower buds compared to the female tree. These large male flower buds are an important winter food for the ruffed grouse. In other words, if you see a grouse in a tree in winter you can be assured that it's perched on a male aspen.

Secondly, aspen grow as *clones*, meaning that a group of trees in one area are probably all growing from the same network of roots. Aspen clones vary widely in extent and can range from a few trees to may thousands of "stems." The genetic differences between clones causes certain groups of trees to turn green in spring at different times. We have one aspen clone on our land that "greens up" quite a bit earlier than the surrounding forest and we eagerly await "her" announcement of spring. The larger clones are usually female.

Poplars and aspens belong to the genus *Populus* which some suggest come from the Roman expression *arbour populii,* meaning "the people's tree." Humans have a curious relationship with the aspen. On one hand the tree has been used by people since time immemorial, but aspen are also viewed by others as a fast growing "weed" tree that can quickly overwhelm yards, pastures, and other more desirable tree species.

Many wood burners across North America look down on the aspen as a source of fuel wood. And while aspen may rank down the list in terms of heat content, it burns well enough to heat thousands of homes on the prairies. Not only that, it is almost the "perfect" firewood tree. It grows straight and tall with little change in diameter plus there are few branches until you get to the top of the tree, making cutting the limbs quite convenient. Finally, when challenged by "firewood snobs" regarding the heating characteristics of aspen, I need only remind them about aspen's history during pioneer times as the fuel wood that carried prairie settlers through some of the coldest winters on earth. Not bad for a "waste tree."

The trembling aspen is without a doubt the most "wildlife-friendly" tree in the forest. Moose, elk, and deer "browse" on the tender tips of the young trees, and the snowshoe hares nibble on any green branch that happens to fall on the forest floor. Indeed it is standard practice in Newfoundland, where hunting and gathering is a way of life, to make "rabbit gardens" by felling green aspens and making a big pile of the tree tops. The green branches are magnets for hares, and you can now go to your "garden" at leisure and get a rabbit for dinner.

In addition, the aspen is coming into its own as a commercial resource used in the production of "oriented strand board." While some will view this as a negative, the fact that aspen regenerate like crazy after cutting means that forest companies that depend on aspen are creating the kinds of "young forests" that causes wildlife to thrive.

Lastly, aspen are beautiful. A hillside of trembling aspen in summer comes alive during a breeze as the leaves tremble and dance. For me, I can anticipate spring simply by picking a bud from a balsam poplar and crushing it. The balsam odour that is released evokes powerful images of spring and a reminder of the smells that will infuse the forest in a few short months.

Best of the season, and take care of the earth; it's the only one we've got.

Harvesting Poplar

Manitoba Deer Season Provides Many Lessons

(November 2008)

By all accounts Manitoba deer hunters had a pretty good year in terms of animals harvested, but the message in terms of deer numbers was a very mixed bag across the province. The general consensus seems to be that deer numbers have declined across Manitoba since the heydays of the 1990s, but that there were enough deer to make the hunt very challenging and interesting. One landowner in southwestern Manitoba told me that, where he might see a hundred deer in a field during the winter, he now sees fifty or so. Southwestern Manitoba is a traditional deer hunting region, and I'm receiving very consistent reports of expanded coyote populations which could account for reduced deer numbers. I spent the middle Saturday of the rifle deer season in the Virden area hunting with my son-in-law, and we did see many coyote tracks and even spooked a few of these "brush wolves" during the hunt. But to be fair we did see many deer tracks and over the course of that day saw about fifteen animals overall. Which isn't too bad.

Coyote numbers are approaching levels where they are beginning to become problems in terms of livestock depredation. The Manitoba Agricultural Services Corporation pays out about $300,000 per year to compensate producers for animals lost to coyotes. In order to reduce the burgeoning populations of this predator, Manitoba Conservation this year for the first time allowed deer hunters to take one coyote while deer hunting. It is not known how many hunters availed themselves of this opportunity but, with some thirty-five to forty *thousand* rifle deer hunters, there could have been quite a few coyotes taken.

GRAHAM AND HIS FIRST DEER

Last Saturday produced a memorable deer hunting experience in that my son-in-law, Graham Street, took his first deer ever. He came to hunting somewhat later than most, but his hunting skill level is expanding at an awesome rate. During the afternoon we were moving quietly and slowly through a wooded pasture on Crown land. This technique, known as "still hunting", is challenging at the best of times given the extreme ability of white-tailed deer to detect a moving hunter. We were about 100 metres apart when a shot from Graham's old .303 British rang out. I stopped, waited for a minute and then moved towards Graham. When I got close enough I could see him on one knee beside a fat fork-horn buck, with his hand on the animal. He looked up at me and I could see he was experiencing the joy and the tragedy of the hunt at the same time. And in his own words:

"I was walking slowly into the wind, moving from bluff to bluff looking, waiting and watching when suddenly I spotted this deer feeding about thirty yards in front of me. His head was down as he fed. Before I knew it, my rifle was up and I was able to place a shot right in the neck. And down he went."

And as we together cleaned the animal and then hauled it out, Graham told me that this experience was one of the most profound of his life. And rightly so; taking an animal's life and taking responsibility for your own food are not trivial experiences. I was very proud; a great hunter and conservationist had just been born.

Spring Hunting Opportunities Abound

(MAY 2007)

It used to be that fall was synonymous with hunting, but not any more. Exploding snow goose populations have necessitated a spring hunt, the introduction of wild turkeys into Manitoba has been a spectacular success culminating in a spring season, and there's always the traditional spring hunt for black bears.

I am especially partial to the spring snow goose hunt, and one April day found me at the southern Manitoba farm of my hunting partner, Ralph Smart. Smart, who had been keeping tabs on the big white geese in his area, called me earlier in the week and said, "You better come down right away. I'm covered in snow geese."

Spring snow geese are quite different from the fall birds. Fall birds seem to spend an inordinate amount of time on the southern prairies fattening up on waste grain for a leisurely southward migration. It's a different story in spring. The increasing day length, called the "photoperiod" by scientists, works its magic on the bird's hormone levels and the urgency to breed results in a rapid northward migration. Snow geese follow close behind the northward advancing "snow line," almost willing the snow to recede in their headlong rush to their ancestral arctic tundra breeding grounds.

It's this aggressive breeding strategy that is both a blessing and a curse for snow geese. Their transcontinental lifestyle allows them to take advantage of the high quality and energy-rich agricultural food supplies which ensures that the birds arrive on the tundra in superb physical condition. Just as an aside, it's these fat reserves that make spring snow geese such great eating!

Body condition is crucial in the harsh arctic climate and a bird in good condition is one that brings off a large clutch of offspring. I'm a believer in the "tipping point" theory of wildlife populations, whereby a species numbers slowly increase up to that point where they achieve that "critical mass" at which point their numbers begin to skyrocket.

Most species of geese in North America are increasing rapidly, and the snow goose is no exception. To illustrate how fast numbers have grown the US Fish and Wildlife Service estimated that the population of Lesser Snow geese increased by three hundred percent from 1969 to 1994, and right now the current population of the birds just in the mid-continent area of North America is estimated to be between 4.5 and 6 million birds. The fragile Canadian arctic, with its short growing season, cannot support populations of that size. For example, large areas of the breeding grounds around Hudson Bay have been denuded of all vegetation by geese through overgrazing, a situation that scientists believe may also be contributing to the decline of breeding populations of other migratory bird species that share the breeding grounds and winter in North America.

To deal with burgeoning snow goose numbers a spring hunting season for "light geese" was initiated in 2000. Limits have been expanded and in Manitoba a hunter can take twenty of the birds per day and have an astonishing eighty birds in possession.

But Mother Nature has a way of dealing with humanity's attempts to "manage" her. And in the case of the snow goose, the species has become quite difficult to hunt under this regime of relentless gunning pressure all along its flyway and during all season of the year. Snow geese travel in huge flocks which are a delight to view but with thousands of "eyes" constantly on the lookout, a hunter is hard pressed to put out enough decoys to lure a big flock or to sneak up on the wary birds.

Smart knows all of the landowners in his area and favours a technique of stationing himself between masses of geese that are feeding and pass shooting the birds as they "trade" between the flocks. This requires mobility and a keen knowledge of goose behaviour. And since Smart has been observing the birds for years he almost knows what a goose will do before it does!

Our two-day hunt was a delight. Not only did we manage to get seventeen nice, plump snow geese, but my Chesapeake, Mountie, was able to get some fine retrieves in after a long winter.

Smart has observed that bald eagles seem to accompany every flock, and he has watched them swoop a flock and pick off any unwary stragglers. In fact, as he pointed out, a flock will flush differently if spooked by an eagle or by hunters. Eagles cause a flock to fly "low and away" while hunters cause a flock to go "straight up."

We did manage to "wrestle" a snow goose from an eagle when Mountie beat one of the big predatory birds to a wounded snow goose. That proved to be just one of the stories from a very memorable snow goose hunt.

Caroline's favourite: Crock Pot Goose

1/2 cup soy sauce
4 tsp canola oil
4 tsp lemon juice
2 tsp Worcestershire sauce
2 cloves of garlic chopped finely
Goose Legs/Breasts
3/4 to 1 cup all purpose flour
1/4 cup butter
1 can (10 3/4 ounce) condensed mushroom soup
1 1/3 cups water

Combine soy sauce, canola oil, lemon juice, Worcestershire sauce and garlic. Pour over goose meat and marinade in plastic bag. Refrigerate for 4 hours or overnight

Discard marinade and toss goose meat in flour. Brown meat in butter on all sides. Transfer to slow cooker.

Combine mushroom soup, water and pour over goose. Cover and cook on high for 5-6 hours or until meat is tender.

A Spring Snow Goose Hunt

Signs of Spring, or You Are What You Eat

(PREVIOUSLY UNPUBLISHED)

March is a great time to observe wildlife and to learn more about the trials and tribulations they must go through in order to survive. The disappearing snow uncovers observational treasures such as moose, deer, and elk droppings (we hunters are always walking with downcast eyes looking for "sign"), which give you an idea of where they spent the winter. I recall one spring when I came across piles of deer sign in a small patch of my woods. This was obviously an over-wintering location where the deer had "yarded up" to sit out a particularly nasty winter.

Just last week, I was walking along one of my trails when I came across some elk tracks. I was able to carefully piece together this particular elk's diet by following him or her for about two hundred metres. This animal had a decided preference for chokecherry twigs. Chokecherries and the other shrub species are collectively referred to as "browse" and are the difference between life or death for most big game. On my place at least, moose really like red osier dogwood (sometimes called red "willow") while deer will go out of their way to browse on the fine twigs of the snowberry.

Spring food getting is not quite so benign when carnivores are involved. Winters can be tough on predators, and many enter spring in bad shape and their hunger drives them to simply "do what predators do." That was brought home to Caroline and me last week while on one of our liberating spring walks through our forest. Our pond was still frozen, and as we approached it, a flock of ravens flushed, a sure sign that there was a kill nearby. Sure enough, there was a bloody patch on the ice surrounded by bits of hide and entrails. And as we got closer, a coyote ran up the hill, carrying a deer leg like a bloody prized possession. It was obvious that a coyote pack had trapped the deer on the ice and made short work of it. And like all hunters from time immemorial, I immediately resented the coyotes for taking one of "my deer;" a silly notion to be sure. Coyotes have to eat too.

And just this afternoon, while coming home from town, I observed four wings flapping about in a stubble field. I quickly trained my binoculars on the birds and watched as a young bald eagle killed a Canada goose that it had obviously just knocked out of the sky. It was a gruesome sight as the eagle, perched on top of the struggling goose, proceeded to yank the feathers from behind the goose's head presumably to bite it behind the neck.

And lastly, my neighbour Don McDonald called a couple of days ago to say that their cat Emma, was no more. McDonald heard a commotion in his yard and was just in time to see a fisher dragging poor Emma into the woods. For some reason fishers have a real "thing" for cats, so if you live in fisher country, be careful with your pets.

INQUISITIVE FISHER ON SHED ROOF

Late October: a Time of Transition

(October 2004)

For many, late October is a depressing time of year. It's truly the end of summer, and the leafless landscape stands in stark contrast to the beautiful September we experienced. In our neighbourhood, south of Riding Mountain National Park, the aspens this year held their leaves longer than ever, covering our rolling countryside with a lingering golden hue. It was truly beautiful.

But late October has a beauty all its own, and the melancholy landscape provides a comforting feeling of well-being. Our wood supply is safely stored away, and the cold room is bulging with jams, jellies, and preserves in spite of this being about the worst gardening year we have ever experienced. Luckily potato grower Ian Wishart was able to provide a big bag of his wonderful Portage Plains potatoes to replace the pitiful crop from our repeatedly frozen garden.

Fresh wild game, of course, is a staple in our household, and what's on the dinner plate usually reflects what's available from the wild. The first fresh game meal of the year is normally the fat little blue wing teal. This tastiest of all ducks is an early migrant, so when Caroline orders up a duck dinner in early September, it's the little "bluies" that I search out. An alternate bird is the sharp-tailed grouse that are much easier to get early in the fall since they are "holed up" in the little bluffs as opposed to later on when they are in big flocks in the open fields and flush long before one gets in shotgun range.

LATE SEASON RUFFED GROUSE

Blue winged teal are all gone by late October but their place is taken by ruffed grouse, the lesser scaup duck (known locally as the "bluebill") and those fat grain-fed mallards so beloved by Prairie waterfowlers. Early in the fall, both duck species are either too skinny or covered with pinfeathers that makes them almost impossible to pluck.

I usually wait to hunt ruffed grouse until the leaves are down and you can see better. This elusive bird is tough enough as it is, so I need all the help I can get! Ruffies are considered by many to be the tastiest of all wild game and are well worth pursuing. I was concerned about ruffed grouse populations given our very wet spring, but I'm seeing an encouraging number. Tough birds.

October 18 was the opening day for hunting deer with muzzleloaders, and we were lucky, but brother Tim was not.

Tim and his son Mark had scouted out some marvellous stands in the Whiteshell. High deer numbers and its proximity to Winnipeg make it an ideal hunting area. Both Tim and Mark are quite taken with the beauty and solitude of the forest in late October.

On the opening Monday, Tim "escaped" from work and was "on stand" before first light. He waited patiently, enjoying the sights and sounds of the forest and was treated to the sight of a northern shrike, one of Canada's rare birds. These are the things that happen when you sit quietly in the forest for hours on end. You "melt" into the habitat and a whole new world opens up.

But business was business and in the late morning two deer showed up. Tim steadied the gun, pulled the trigger and when the smoke cleared; nothing. "How could I miss?" he asked himself. He checked and re-checked the entire area and no sign of anything. Obviously a clean miss. He decided to check out the scope and sure enough a test fire revealed that the gun was about twenty centimetres off at twenty-five metres. He had sighted in his muzzleloader the week before, but it was obvious that the scope had been knocked out of alignment. A lesson for us all. Check your scopes.

After a "deerless" afternoon, he drove back to Winnipeg and saw deer along the road almost all the way to Winnipeg. "It's as if they were mocking me," he said. We've all been there.

Caroline and I had a different experience on opening day. No deer were seen in the morning, but we managed to get our two black powder deer on our own land that evening; a much easier hunt than Tim's, but that's hunting isn't it?

What this means is that I can now get back to my beloved bird hunting. There's no time like late October.

Stories in the Snow

(January 2010)

Well, winter is finally here, and some would say with a vengeance. But so are one of the biggest benefits that winter offers to nature-lovers: animal tracks.

Some of my most rewarding outdoor experiences have been with trappers. These self-taught outdoors professionals are highly educated in the ways of animals. One seasoned trapper told me, "It's through animal tracks that I get to understand nature." The information these pros can milk from a set of tracks leaves me in awe.

Though my skills are more limited, I've learned at least as much about animal habits from tracks as I have from direct observations. For example, moose often reside on my land, but are rarely seen. During a January moose hunt, I came to realize that the animal I was following was not zig-zagging aimlessly. Rather, it traveled from one dogwood bush to another, browsing one down before moving to the next. I have encountered evidence of this food preference many times since.

And speaking of the deer family, winter is when they switch to a diet of browse, which is the growth from last summer on shrubs such as hazel, willow, and young aspens in addition to the dogwood mentioned above. The tips of newly browsed shrubs will be white as opposed to "old" browse tips which will be weathered by the rains and winds of summer.

An "open" November means that Caroline and I can bring in our winter's wood supply. The lack of snow and frozen ground in late November is perfect for tree hauling. Our yard is now graced with a pile of eighty limbed poplar trees just waiting to be cut and split, a pleasant winter chore if there ever was one. Incidentally, we hauled out our trees with "Little Red," a 1952 vintage W4 International tractor. Imagine that, a machine that still does an honest day's work in spite of its fifty-two years of service. "They sure don't make them like they used to," applies in spades to Little Red!

Animal tracks help keep me aware of what's new or changing. About ten years ago, I encountered a large, round track on top of the snow. I knew right away that a lynx had moved in, but I didn't actually spot an animal until some time later. Same thing for fisher, a larger member of the mink family and one of the few predators that actively hunts for porcupine. I have been noticing their tracks for awhile but only recently have I started to see them regularly.

But now the snow is starting to come, and while some species struggle with deep snows, others thrive. Take the ruffed grouse, a noble and tough game bird if ever there was one. This hardy winter resident takes advantage of deep snows by diving into snow banks to spend the night. Not only does this hide them from most predators, the snow acts like an insulating blanket. If you have a keen eye you can spot the entry hole in the snow before the bird detects you, and you can thrill to the bird bursting out of its den. The difference in temperature can range from minus forty at the surface to just below freezing close to the ground, giving the ruffed grouse and other animals protection from bitter weather. While on a ski trip not long ago, I noticed a grouse den right beside the trail. I could see where the bird went in, but not where it exited. Without thinking much about it, I pushed a pole into the hole, only to have the frantic bird explode from the snow! I'm not sure who was more surprised, but the grouse definitely had the sharper end of the encounter.

Ruffed grouse are a personal favourite, and I like to keep track of them on my property. By the middle of December, birds that I've watched from my kitchen window on the forest edge simply vanish. If I go for a ski down the hill and slog through the spruce and tamarack swamp, tracks and other tell-tale signs tell me they've settled in for the winter. Heavy cover gives grouse two important advantages: wind protection and soft snow.

So if we have a long, cold winter and the snow pack lingers, instead of lamenting the long time until spring, try a late-season ski or snowshoe trip. The track-hunting is sure to be excellent.

A Life **Outdoors**

Stories in the Snow

Hunting Reflections

(November 2008)

It has been a very fine hunting year. There's still some hunting left. Caroline has an elk tag for our area starting on December 30, so we'll see if she's able to augment the venison supply with a nice fat elk.

The hearty bird hunters out there have been after ruffed grouse. In my neck of the woods we've got a skiff of snow which allows you to track grouse. Molly and I just walk the trails until we come across a fresh track, and I send Molly in after it. Half the time I get a nice shot. This time of year the ruffies are eating almost straight aspen buds with the odd rose hip and snowberry thrown in.

I thought this was going to be Molly's last year, but she surprised me by getting stronger and stronger as the year went on. She's just charging through those grouse thickets these days.

I was thinking about this year's waterfowl hunting, which was a great success. I like to hunt waterfowl quietly, with a minimum of fanfare, and in areas that others have overlooked. To me that means heading for what I call the "small waters." What do I mean by "small waters?" Well, these are the tiny creeks and small ponds that you can find all over the Manitoba landscape. These areas are often overlooked by traditional waterfowlers who more often than not head for the grain fields after mallards and geese or set up the 100+ decoy spreads on the big marshes like Netley or Delta.

These smaller places are often tucked away in the woods and at the ends of fields and can only be found by the diligent waterfowler who is prepared to travel and scout. But I love to drive Manitoba's back roads, so this type of scouting is certainly not a hardship for me. As a bonus you might find a new grouse covert or a hidden deer trail that just might give you a chance at a nice buck later on.

WATERFOWL HUNTER AT SUNSET

So, you've found the small water, and there's a few ducks milling about. Now what? Well for one thing, small waters need small equipment and few decoys, eight is plenty. And often you can drive close to the water's edge so hauling is minimized. One thing I learned after 35+ years of waterfowling is that the duck situation changes on a daily and even hourly basis. What looks like a near empty sky over a creek at noon can become a buzzing "river of ducks" just before dark. I especially love mornings on small creeks. That wonderful sound of running water is often mixed with the swish of wings as yet unseen waterfowl fly along the watercourse. But as the light rises, look out!

Another bonus about small waters early in the year is that the hunt is warm, out of the wind, safe for kids, and there's a diversity of duck species. Blue-wing teal are my favourite eating duck (our family nickname for them is "supper duck") and small waters can provide teal in abundance. In fact, early on in the fall, I won't let my companions shoot mallards (too many pinfeathers), a discipline that often leaves them gaping in awe as we let mallard after mallard land in the decoys and then fly away. Teal, as a bonus, are delightfully easy to prepare.

I recall one hunt two years ago that my friend Harry put together. He assured me there were birds on the creek, and I eagerly took him up on his offer. We drove to the creek, threw in our decoys and, as the sun rose, were treated to one of the nicest waterfowling experiences I've ever had. We took six different species, with blue-wing teal being number one in the bag. Molly brought in every bird to hand. Harry's passed on now, but it is a memory of him that I will always cherish along with the pictures.

Even if winter's in full swing, why not start thinking about next fall. Get yourself a good supply of topographic maps and start looking for those small creeks and waterbodies for next fall. Once spring comes you'll have a great excuse to look around. So when the time comes, get out there, travel and scout the back roads and, who knows, you just might find your own slice of heaven on the "small waters."

Unique Wildlife Experiences a Part of Country Living

(MARCH 2005)

Living "in the bush" has a number of real advantages. Peace, quiet and beautiful landscapes are some of them but unique wildlife experiences surely rank right at the top.

Why just last week Caroline remarked that the screen in our gazebo had, for some strange reason, ripped apart. It had been quite windy so I assumed that my homemade creation had finally succumbed to the elements. Thinking nothing of it, I took Mountie, our Chesapeake Bay Retriever, for a walk. But upon our return he started to run around the gazebo in quite an excited state. *Darn squirrel must've ripped the screen,* I thought. *And I've got to get rid of him.*

But just at that point Caroline, who had looked out the kitchen window wondering what all the fuss was about, yelled, "Bob, there's a ruffed grouse in the gazebo!" She'd seen the bird beating itself against the other screen. Well that solved the mystery of the torn screen but now what?

Mountie was quickly kennelled and then I slowly opened the door of the building. Dead quiet inside. Obviously the bird was frozen, hoping I'd just go away. A quick search revealed the frightened bird behind a cardboard box and he (it was a male judging by the tail feather colouration) was easily captured. After a few close up pictures, this "bird in the hand" was released to become that proverbial "bird in the bush."

A couple of years before, Caroline was on the phone by our big kitchen window. She happened to look out just in time to see a full-grown lynx stroll out of the bush, right by said gazebo referred to above. The big cat lay down directly under the window and proceeded to groom himself. After the job was completed, he picked himself up and, moving gracefully as only a cat can, melted back into the woods. Caroline still talks about that one.

There were a lot of bears around the Riding Mountain area last summer. One day, while I was writing a column actually, Mountie started barking as if someone had driven into the yard. I went upstairs, let him out, and looked into the yard. Nothing. At that point I caught a movement out of the corner of my eye. I turned just in time to see a bear stroll around the corner of the house right on our deck. So there I am at the front door, Mountie's at the base of the stairs, and the bear nearly at my right elbow. A tricky triangle if I ever saw one. As I yelled for Mountie to get back inside (luckily he listened) the bear ran back on the deck and around the house. I quickly closed the door and raced to the sliding glass door just in time to go nose-to-nose with one really frightened bear. He dashed back around the house and down the steps, upsetting one of Caroline's flower pots. But both the flowers and the bear survived.

Nathan Sims farms with his family near MacGregor and relayed this wildlife story. He was watching a crow chase a kestrel, which is a very small hawk about the size of a robin. Sims figured that the crow was after the hawk's eggs. But the kestrel had other ideas and just as the crow was closing in the tiny hawk flew straight up, over, around, and landed right on the crows back! Just like a fighter pilot outfoxing a pursuing plane.

"There were black feathers everywhere as the hawk scratched and bit that old crow," said Sims. "That crow took off like a scalded cat!"

But the topper has to go to my neighbour Candy Irwin who, along with her husband Jim, operates an eco-tourism company. But she arrived at "the ranch" as Jim's new bride very much a city girl. And in her own words:

"It was January, and I had been married to Jim for about six months. It was real cold, and as I pulled my little "city car" into the machine shed there was a real commotion overhead. And before I knew what was what there was a loud "thump" on the roof of the car. All I saw at first was a black and white bloody mess. When I looked closer, it turned out to be a headless skunk with most of his guts torn out! I jumped back just in time to see a great horned owl swooping down right at me, big eyes blazing. I think he just wanted to escape, but I hit the shop floor anyway. And then a second owl came out and scooped up their "prize" and headed for the woods. I ran into the house to tell Jim, and after I was finished the story he just grinned and said, "Welcome to the country, Honey."

Indeed.

A Manitoba Artisan

(February 2008)

One year, I had the opportunity to attend the Toronto Hunting and Outdoors Show. When I wasn't manning Delta Waterfowl's booth, I wandered through the displays, just like a kid in a candy store. A knife-maker's booth caught my eye, and after looking over his wares and swapping hunting stories I asked the proprietor, "Say, do you know my friend Charlie Niedermayer from Manitoba?"

"Know him!" he exclaimed. "Charlie's one of the finest knife makers in Canada and his work is legendary!" I smiled, because as the proud owner of eight Niedermayer knives, I feel the same way.

Charlie Niedermayer lives in Powerview, Manitoba, and is one of those natural craftsmen who takes pieces of wood, metal, bone, or leather and combines them into knives that are simply works of art. His work is inspired by nature, and he views his knife making as "a part of hunting, which I love." Charlie started making knives in the 1970s, producing one a year to take with him on his moose hunting adventures. "I tried to improve my knives every year by using better materials and designs," he said.

Others took notice of his knives, and what started as a hobby quickly became a small business. His basement workshop has cutters, grinders, buffers, and a heat-treating furnace where he tempers the finest modern steel for his knives. He constantly researches new techniques and designs and uses exotic materials such as antlers, musk ox horn, warthog tusks and tropical hardwoods like "coco-bolo" and "Australian black hair."

The knife making and knife collecting world is one of those vast sub-cultures that exist in our society. Charlie is "collected" by a number of aficionados, and his knives can be found in all the provinces of Canada, the Arctic, as well as in the United States, Germany, Scotland, and even Africa. Charlie makes "working knives" and, as he puts it, "I expect my knives to be used and not sit on the shelf."

Well, Charlie, you should be happy with me since I'm never far from my eight "Niedermayers" which are used for field dressing big game, skinning, cleaning birds, and filleting fish. Each of my knives is different, and they feel alive in my hands as I experience the skill and thought that went into each design. "It is important that the knife design match the purpose," said Charlie. I like my fish filleting knife so much that I volunteer to clean everyone's fish on our many angling adventures.

But, don't think that you can just buy a Niedermayer knife and that's that. No sir. Charlie makes sure that you buy the knife designed to fit the intended purpose plus he provides advice on the sharpening and care of your knife. You basically "adopt" a Niedermayer knife as opposed to buying it. I recall field dressing a moose with one of Charlie's knives and, in a fit of overzealousness, used my knife to cut up the breastbone, a "no-no" if there ever was one. The knife did the job but I nicked it in a few places. I really didn't want to tell Charlie but when he came to visit me this summer I reluctantly showed him the damaged knife. He shook his head, sighed at my carelessness, and said, "Give it to me Bob, and I'll fix it." Well he had it back to me as good as new in time for the fall because, as he wrote in his note, "I knew that you wanted her back by your side in time for the hunting season." Note the personalization of his knives.

A few years ago Charlie decided to take up wood carving and was actually working on a life-sized red-tailed hawk when I called. Like all master craftsmen he is a success at whatever he tries. Just last April at the Prairie Canada Wood Carvers Show he took Best-of-Show (novice class), Best of Division, and the People's Choice award for a life sized carving of a ruffed grouse. This carving is a stunning piece of work and rivals any of the art that I've seen illustrated in any sporting magazine, including the publication of the Ruffed Grouse Society of North America.

Charlie's knives reflect his love of hunting and the outdoors. "To me hunting means being outside with good company experiencing nature and the wilderness. Even though I didn't always get a moose, all of my hunts were successful because I thoroughly enjoyed my time in the woods."

Niedermayer has been a hunter all of his life, and on the occasion of his 80th birthday, his wife Christine insisted that he go out moose hunting with "the boys."

"I've been a moose hunter for years, and I really like the early season," said Niedermayer. "It's usually nice weather, and you can experience the thrill of calling bull moose."

Never one to shy away from a challenge, Niedermayer told me that he recently switched from being a right-handed shooter to being a left-handed one."

"My right eye isn't as good as my left any more, so I had to switch sides," he said. "It is very important to me to be a top notch shot since the last thing I want to do is wound an animal. I have too much respect for them."

His hunt with "the boys" sounded like a dream come true. First the crew flew from Bissett to a lake in the Bloodvein River area. After they unloaded the float plane, their first task was to make their old moose camp livable. And then things took a decided turn for the better.

"Just as we finished setting up camp at around three o'clock in the afternoon we heard a bull moose grunt about seventy-five yards away," recounted Niedermayer. "We couldn't believe our luck! Moose are often attracted to noises, and I guess the sounds of us making camp brought this one in. And then, wonder of wonders, we heard even more grunting throughout the night. You better believe that we were excited!"

But all hunters have to be mindful of that old saying; "that's why they call it hunting and not getting!" Niedermayer went on to describe the next day.

"My partner and I paddled five miles up the lake to a creek mouth only to find the place flooded out," he described. "We couldn't go anywhere so we backtracked towards camp and called and hunted around there for the rest of the week and didn't hear a single animal!"

Niedermayer and his crew worked hard all that week. But nothing worked. Niedermayer was not worried in the least.

"It was a wonderful week of moose hunting," he said. "The sights, sounds, and smells of the land brought back a flood of memories; memories of canoe trips gone by; memories of tea made with clear, clean creek water; memories of great companions telling stories. It was a memorable hunt! I was right at home. I belong here in the wilderness."

Charlie Niedermayer is an inspiration to us all. He's a man driven by the search for perfection yet is humbled by the wonders of nature. He doesn't know if he'll be able to go out moose hunting again, but he will continue to be inspired by his family, his art, and his appreciation for the natural world. And he will inspire the rest of us as well.

Charlie Niedermayer reflects a different time and era. In a time of gigantic egos and instant gratification, Charlie's works are timeless and his modesty humbling. He joked with me and said, "Now Bob, don't build me up too much, I still want to keep knife making as a hobby." Frankly, that's hard to do given the skill and pride that go into every knife.

While Charlie's carvings are not for sale, he does have a limited supply of knives on hand, any one of which would make the gift of a lifetime for the hunter on your Christmas list. Charlie Niedermayer of Powerview—hunter, master craftsman and a Manitoba treasure.

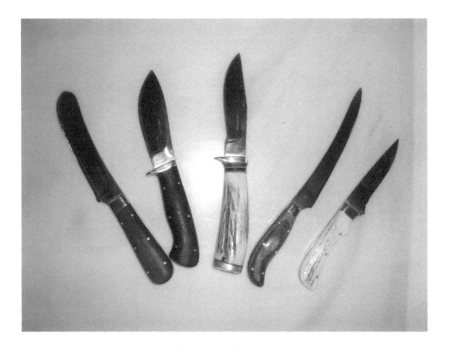

Charlie's Knives

A Man for All Seasons

(June 2009)

I have a real soft spot for individuals who stand out, not only for their inherent talent, but for their determination to go against the grain and live life on their own terms. South of Riding Mountain National Park in the Sandy Lake area lives one such man. Seventy-five-year-old Ernie Sichewski lives on the shores of a beautiful lake and probably knows more about wildlife than anyone I've ever met. Sichewski's knowledge is not of the theoretical kind, but is based on the wisdom of experience as befits one of eleven children born and raised in modest circumstances on a small "pioneer" farm.

"My chore was to milk cows, by hand, before I ran all the way to our one-room school," he reminisced. "And on the way home, I would check my trap-line and, if I caught anything, sell the fur to earn some extra money."

This was the way of life back then and is within the living memory of my older neighbours. Sichewski left home at age fifteen and worked on the railroad for a number of years. He also raced snowmobiles and even built one from scratch! He was such a successful racer that he won sixty-two trophies and then decided to, you guessed it, go into the trophy business! But his heart was always in the country, and in 1995, he left Winnipeg for good and moved "back home."

"I never lost my love of nature no matter where I traveled. If I had my way, I'd sleep in the bush!" he joked. "The freedom and satisfaction that comes from spending nearly every day in the outdoors is very important to me."

ERNIE WITH TAME RUFFED GROUSE

Sichewski specializes in trapping problem wildlife such as coyotes that prey on livestock and beavers that plug culverts and cause flooding.

"From 1999 to today, I've taken about 4,400 beavers and will probably end up with over 6,000 before this year is over," he noted. "But I skin and sell every one of them since I don't believe in wasting these animals."

Spending a lot of time "in the bush" means that you increase the probability of encountering wildlife, and some of those encounters can be downright remarkable. Take "Puykie," Sichewski's "tame" ruffed grouse. In his own words:

"In June of 2008, I was driving my tractor to pick up a load of wood. I saw this grouse with three little ones. Later in June, I saw her again but with no little ones: I guess a hawk had taken them. In October she showed up again while I was cutting firewood. She got real close and one time jumped on the logs I had piled in the wagon. She seemed to be attracted by the sound of engines or the logs knocking against each other; who knows? Eventually she would run alongside the quad. Once I stopped and shuffled my feet in the leaves and she jumped at me like she was playing. It was then she got really friendly and I began feeding her high bush cranberries by hand since I knew grouse liked them. And finally she would jump on the handlebars of my quad to get fed and ride around a little bit. It was amazing!"

Now ruffed grouse are notoriously difficult to tame or hand feed and numerous scientific experiments have failed. These birds normally live on their own with little help from humans and I have never heard of a ruffed grouse doing what this one did. Which makes Sichewski's experience all the more remarkable.

"I called her "Puykie" after the sound she makes; or at least that's what it sounds like to me," Sichewski said.

He went on to say, "You know, I've killed hundreds of grouse in my day; mostly to feed me and my family. But after my experience with "Puykie" I really don't want to kill another one."

And frankly, who can blame him.

A Manitoba Conservation Pioneer

(JULY 2004)

Manitoba has some very special places. Our parks, wildlife management areas, Conservation Districts, and forest reserves protect and manage some of Manitoba's most precious natural resources and are enjoyed by all; never more than at this time of year. In addition, governments at all levels have put into place great public works that provide flood protection, deliver water for towns, industries, and agriculture, and ensure that we have efficient transportation networks.

You probably thank the "powers that be" that someone had the foresight to establish all of this, but that's usually as far as it goes. But as you marvel at the great flocks of geese at Oak Hammock or enjoy a day in a wildlife management area, or partake of any of our beautiful places, or take solace in the Floodway, you really should stop to thank those who had the wisdom to make this all happen. I'd like to tell you about one such person; my old friend, hunting buddy, and mentor, Ted Poyser.

I met Ted Poyser in 1984 while I was living on the farm and doing some environmental consulting work "on the side." He was looking for a fisheries biologist to conduct a study in the Northwest Territories as part of a larger project. Was I interested? You bet I was. That first venture blossomed into what is now twenty-year friendship and mentorship that I treasure. Let me share some of that.

Poyser was born on the family farm near MacGregor, Manitoba, in 1927. The farm had been settled by his grandfather in 1888, and the pioneer memories were still strong. Of course, he had his own hardships to contend with such as the Great

Depression which had engulfed the entire Prairies. Model T cars, wood cutting bees, horses and sleighs, and one-room schoolhouses were all part of his upbringing. Makes you realize how far technology has come in one lifetime!

This "grounding" on the farm, coupled with strong academic abilities, propelled him to attain a Masters degree in Agriculture from the University of Manitoba in 1950 and then careers over the next forty years with both the federal and provincial governments. Poyser's first job was conducting soil and land surveys across Manitoba, and it was here, as he says that "I began to see the vision of the Manitoba landscape as a continuous mantle of soil formed from the variety of climatic, geological, hydrological, and botanical processes." This vision would stand him in good stead.

Travelling to and from hunting and fishing spots with Poyser is an education in geomorphology as he describes the various processes that created our beautiful and productive Prairie landscape.

Fortunately for Manitobans, all of his expertise was put to good use, and as Poyser rose through the ranks he was given more and more responsibilities over land and resource management. The 1960s and 1970s were especially active times for Poyser during the Premierships of Duff Roblin and Ed Schreyer where he participated at the highest levels. He views his time with Roblin with special affection and states that, "Duff Roblin was the planner and architect of Manitoba as we enjoy it today." Now while politicians quite rightly take the credit for initiatives, they must rely on dedicated civil servants to carry out their grand visions; and here is where Poyser excelled.

Some of the projects that he directed included assembling the lands for Bird's Hill and Spruce Woods Provincial Parks, as well as planning the development at Oak Hammock Marsh. In addition he was able to assist with the purchase of lands to greatly expand Manitoba's network of Wildlife Management Areas. The Floodway, road networks, and Conservation Districts are but a few of the other initiatives Poyser worked on in his remarkable career.

Apart from wildlife and parks, Poyser's other great interest has always been soil and water conservation on agricultural lands. He's especially proud of the Conservation District movement that combines local farm knowledge with the capability to improve agricultural conservation practises. Similarly, as the Chair of the Manitoba Habitat Heritage Corporation, he oversaw an expansion of its work in the areas of wetlands conservation and riverbank protection.

Poyser loved working with farmers. He recalls planting trees on some fragile land north of Neepawa, described in his published essay "Planting Trees on a Hill." After some discussion, the farmer agreed that planting trees on a steep slope that kept washing away was probably a good idea. Shortly after he and Poyser started planting, they were interrupted by the farmer's pioneer mother who was quite agitated at the thought of a new forest on the same hill that her and her husband had so labouriously cleared by hand many decades before! "Who needs more trees?" she thundered. Poyser prevailed and there's now a forest on that hillside.

I'm looking forward to many more hunting and fishing trips with my friend Ted Poyser. We can all count on the fingers of one hand the truly remarkable people who have changed our lives. He is one of them. Think about that the next time you enjoy one of Manitoba's great places. Chances are Ted Poyser made it that way.

Ted Poyser and Ruffed Grouse

A Passion for Waterfowling

(August 2010)

Biologist, renowned medical researcher, ardent waterfowl conservationist, passionate duck hunter, Ducks Unlimited Canada (DUC) Emeritus Director, boat builder, ace decoy carver, and witness to World War 2; well no one can say that seventy-six-year-old Dr. Frank Baldwin hasn't led an eventful and productive life. And with what he has "on his plate," decades of accomplishments await this remarkable Manitoban.

Baldwin was raised in rural England on an East Anglia farm just thirty miles from the French coast.

"Our farming practices were quite traditional," described Baldwin. "There was lots of wildlife habitat, so hunting and shooting just came naturally. And it was on this farm that I learned the great lessons of sportsmanship, marksmanship, stewardship, and conservation. My father saw to that!

"Our farm was on the flight path of the German bombers," he continued. "So for a while during World War 2, until we were evacuated to a safer area in the UK, crashing planes, dogfights, and jettisoned bombs are some of my most vivid childhood memories."

After the war, and after experiencing the London Blitz, Baldwin's family returned to the farm. Baldwin became increasingly fascinated with ecology and wildlife biology and started conducting his own creative style of research.

"When I was fourteen I did a paper on the biology of bomb craters," he explained. "There were hundreds of them in our area and, after the craters filled with water, all manner of plants and animals soon colonized them. I remember my "study crater" quite vividly since the tail of a "doodlebug" bomb was sticking out of the middle of it!"

DR. FRANK BALDWIN DUCK HUNTING

After taking degrees in botany, zoology, and comparative anatomy, Baldwin diverged into the fields of neurology and cell biology where he earned his Doctorate. His researches took him to London, Australia, New Zealand, Saskatchewan, and finally Manitoba. He always found time to experience local waterfowling, and to date has hunted on all continents except South America. And all the while he has maintained a hunting journal that describes each and every hunt he has been on over those sixty-four years.

In 1981, and in the spirit of "giving back" to the ducks, Baldwin spearheaded the formation of the Winnipeg Committee of DUC. Not content with that, he became the founding Chair of the Selkirk DUC Committee and was soon a Senior Volunteer with DUC helping to establish committees all across the Interlake. Baldwin was on the Board of DUC for sixteen years and returned to the Board three years ago as an Emeritus Director with a special interest in youth education.

"I feel strongly that hunters must be involved in wildlife conservation and pass that ethic on to future generations of waterfowl hunters," he explained. "We must also pressure governments at every level to make habitat conservation, especially wetlands, a top priority."

Baldwin is a waterfowl traditionalist who loves to hunt diving ducks on "big water" using well-trained and hardy Labrador Retrievers. He makes his own duck hunting boats and carves his own decoys. By his estimate he's carved hundreds of decoys for himself and friends

Baldwin has also bred a fine line of waterfowl dogs known as "Barclay Labradors." These fine British Labs are world-renowned and in great demand.

And if that isn't enough, Baldwin's son, Frank Jr., is currently Manitoba's Provincial Waterfowl Biologist. So with the Baldwin family on the case, Manitoba's waterfowling and conservation traditions are in good hands indeed.

Sadly, since this column was written, Dr. Frank Baldwin has passed on. But his legacy will live forever.

My Favourite Country Store

(June 2009)

Life in the 21st century has its rewards, but the flip side of modern life is that we always seem to be in a hurry, so much so that we often miss life's hidden treasures. And one of those is the Olha General Store in the community of Olha just south of Riding Mountain National Park. Olha is one of many Prairie settlements that thrived during settlement times but have faded away due to school consolidation, centralization, and the general withering of small-scale agriculture. One by one these iconic little communities, with their memories and histories, are winking out as the modern world rushes by. Olha was officially open-for-business in 1908 with the opening of the Post Office, but the Olha General Store, a beautifully restored church, and a community hall are all that remain.

Steve and Marion Koltusky have been running the store for thirty-eight years and are assisted today by their nineteen year old son Ryan, who is also a student at Assiniboine Community College. The Olha General Store is a favourite stopping point for backroads travellers, hunters, and anglers not to mention the local farm folk; many of whom will shop nowhere else. The Olha General Store seems to be from another time. In addition to the staples of flour, bread, eggs, and milk, the shelves are stocked with all manner of country goods from snacks for the road, to garlic sausage, to bricks of cheese, and other odds and ends that a country traveller might require. Hunting and fishing licenses, must-haves at any country store, are available for purchase.

And there's always Marion behind the counter ready to provide travellers with information, country wisdom, local news, and of course reports on the progress of local crops, pastures, and haylands. Marion and Steve also look after the beautiful Olha Church and will proudly take visitors on tours. The paintings alone are worth the tour.

MARION AT OLHA STORE

"I have moved three times in my entire life, but I've never left this section of land," she laughed. "We love running the store, what with all the interesting people and good friends who stop by. We won't get rich but we cherish this way of life."

Steve and Marion also farm five quarters of land with Ryan helping whenever he is home from school. Steve has decided to use alfalfa rotations and has eliminated all chemical use on their land.

"Wildlife is very important to us, which is why we have left a lot of bush on our land," Marion explained. "Just yesterday there were fourteen elk near our garden, and I do hope they leave my plants alone. But Steve and Ryan have elk tags so one may end up in our freezer."

The Koltusky family exemplifies sustainability. From the big garden to the wild game in the freezer this is one family that can adapt to just about anything the world can dish out. And being able to make their own way in the world is very important to them. A wall poster in the Olha General Store says it all:

"*I believe in the dignity of labour, whether with head or hand; that the world owes no man a living, but that it owes every man an opportunity to make a living.*"

Do yourself a favour and stop in at the Olha General Store. You'll be glad you did.

A Call to a Neighbour

(August 2000)

We'd had a fine first day home after a trip to Calgary to visit the kids. It was a good trip, and I even got two days of fly fishing with an old friend. We did all of those chores you normally do after a trip. Caroline and I were just sitting down to a supper of moose steak and home-grown potatoes, complemented with a bottle of home made wine; a typical country meal.

Then the phone rang. Caroline answered. Her face clouded; she handed me the phone and said, "It's Candy. She's crying and wants to talk to you." Candy and Jim are our neighbours who run a guest ranch. I took the phone from Caroline. "Bob, it's Stormy," Candy sobbed. "He's down and can't get up. He's in real pain. We've tried everything but its no use. Jim and I can't do it, but could you come over and put him out of his misery?" Stormy was Candy's favourite horse.

I exhaled slowly, knowing that I could not refuse, but also knowing this was something that I'd rather not do. I said, "Sure Candy. When do you want me there?"

"Could you come now," she pleaded. I could. It's the country code; if a neighbour needs you, you go, period.

"Trouble at Jim and Candy's," I told Caroline. "Stormy can't stand up any more, and they've asked me to put him down. They can't do it."

"Well," she said. "I guess you've got to do it." Yeah.

I went to the gun room, unlocked it, and reached for my .30-06. I slipped some shells into my pocket and walked to the truck.

I thought about it on the short drive to their place. Normally, I'm indifferent to horses. I prefer hunting dogs, and I've got a dandy in Molly, my Chesapeake Bay Retriever. She's been my faithful hunting partner for ten falls (hunting dog time is measured in "falls" not "years"). In that time she's broken ice to fetch ducks, flushed pheasants from Montana prairies, and brought back fifteen-pound Canada geese. She guards the house, is company for Caroline, and walked the kids to the school bus as they were growing up. A real friend. Candy and Jim feel as strongly about their horses as I do about Molly. This comparison focused for me what I was about to do. In a strange way I felt honoured. Their respect for me was evident in the fact that they asked me to do this very serious thing.

I drove up their drive and saw the other horses. Was it my imagination or were they all looking toward the corral where I knew Stormy lay? It was a cold and dull day. I pulled into the yard and saw Candy, standing forlornly, watching me. She's a real animal lover, takes in strays, and is the one the neighbours turn to if they have an animal they don't need. I probably imagined it, but she seemed to give me an accusing look as if asking me what I was doing there. Yeah, that's me alright, the Grim Reaper in the Peaceable Kingdom.

I slung the Parker Hale over my shoulder and walked up to her. Candy's normally bright and expressive eyes were red with tears.

"Sorry, Candy," I said and gave her a hug as she sobbed. "Did you say your goodbyes?" I asked.

"Yes," she said in a small voice. "Here's Jim. He'll take you to him. Could you let me get into the house first? I don't want to hear the shot." Sure.

Jim greeted me in a subdued way and we walked into the nearby corral. Stormy was lying on his side and, upon hearing us, tried to rise but couldn't. Jim stood behind me. Their pet goat walked up to me but, unusual for him, he just looked at me. He normally tries to butt you. Guess he knew something different was happening. I looked at Stormy and shook my head.

"Ready, Jim?" I asked. He nodded.

I placed the muzzle by Stormy's ear and pulled the trigger. The report shattered the still air. Hooves pounded in the distance and I saw the horses running hard to the far pasture, spooked by the blast. Stormy's legs stiffened. His last breath steamed from his flaring nostrils. Quickly, though, his legs relaxed as the body shut down.

I looked back at Jim and he gave a curt nod. It was done. I ejected the spent shell and slung the rifle on my shoulder and we walked out.

"Want to come in for some Crown Royal?" Jim asked. Yeah, sound's good.

In the house, Candy was talking to Caroline on the phone. Caroline's comforting words were working, and Candy was looking a little better. They kept talking as Jim poured the whiskey. Candy hung up the phone, joined us and said, "Caroline's coming over." We all sat around, like neighbours do after something like this and we talked. Even laughed a bit as Candy told how Stormy taught her to ride by *not* obeying when Candy gave not quite perfect signals to the horse. Candy soon learned.

We finished up and drove home. I reflected that in spite of miracle technologies, MTV values, a video game culture, and the shallowness of most modern discourse, certain ironclad rules still apply. There is certainty, truth exists, neighbours are important, life is truly beautiful, and death takes all of us eventually. My fiftieth birthday is coming up, and while I expect at least thirty more years, it's a milestone that gets you thinking.

As I got out of my truck in the yard, Molly came bounding up. No matter what happens, your dog is always glad to see you. As I scratched behind her ears I wondered what I would do when the time came for me to make a call to a neighbour.

On Having a Hunting Dog

(March 2010)

My big Chesapeake Bay Retriever Mountie was a speck in the water as he pursued the wounded duck. I had sent him out on a blind retrieve, i.e. one where he goes on faith, not having seen the bird fall. Every now and then he'd look back at me, and I would fling my arm straight up in the air and yell, "Back!" He'd turn around and resume his "dogged" pursuit. Eventually he saw the bird and after a fast and furious chase grabbed the duck and brought him the three hundred metres back to the blind. All my hunting companion could say was, "Well, I'll be; I have never seen anything like it." Hunting with a good dog creates those memorable moments.

My "dog days" started with the kids who said they wanted a dog on the farm where we lived. And with a busy work schedule I was a bit leery, but eventually Caroline and I gave in. But I did stipulate that it had to be a hunting dog; preferable one of the retrieving breeds. I reasoned that maybe I'd get some hunting in with the dog.

That's how we ended up with Molly, a female Chesapeake Bay Retriever. And this was one case where the kids were right. Pretty soon Molly settled in as part of the family and quickly adapted to farm life. I'm partial to the retrieving breeds. They are tractable and, more importantly, trainable. The pointing and flushing breeds need a lot more training to bring out their natural instincts but bringing back birds is what retrievers do. Throw in a good nose and a decent retriever will bring a bird back in almost any situation. Training Molly from her puppy phase to maturity was fun; we basically trained each other. We worked on basic retrieves, blind retrieves, and multiple retrieves. Hand signals and whistle training was next. Upland bird training was next, and she basically picked that up on her own. We'd go for walks in the woods, and if she'd get the scent of a ruffed grouse, she'd chase it. The bird would flush, and if I shot it, her retrieving instincts took over she would bring it to me. She figured out to hunt close to me knowing that a close flush meant a greater likelihood of a retrieve.

Molly was killed in an accident at the age of eleven, and grief engulfed me and our entire family. I didn't know that I could get that emotional about a dog. But when you lose your hunting partner, you are flooded with the memories of hunts past, but death has robbed you of the opportunity to make more.

Our second dog was Mountie, another Chesapeake, who we obtained as a fully trained eighteen-month-old. His owner, Steve, was a kindly man but as a field trial perfectionist he wanted Mountie to obey hand signals at three hundred yards; and not "only" at one hundred yards. Well few bird retrieves are longer than one hundred yards, so when Steve called, I was interested! Best decision I ever made! Mountie took to farm life like a duck to water. Both Molly and Mountie had a deep hatred for bears and nothing would get each dog growling like a bear around the yard, and many a time bears would hightail it out of our farmyard with a Chesapeake close behind.

Mountie is our gentle boy. He has never snapped or growled at anybody and is a great joy for our little granddaughter Eden. She feeds and coos over him. She loves to give Mountie the "sit" command, and she squeals with delight when this gentle giant obeys.

Mountie is a tough dog as befits his breed. The Chesapeake Bay Retriever was bred for the tough conditions on Chesapeake Bay during the great market hunting days of the late 1800s. And to see Mountie break ice to grab a duck or go swimming among the spring ice flows just for the joy of it makes you appreciate just how tough these dogs are.

The partnership between a hunter and his dog becomes more intense over time. With enough time in the field together, each partner soon knows what the other is thinking. Hunting ruffed grouse with Mountie is a perfect example. Mountie trots in front of me, nose in the air. He's relaxed but alert. But as soon as he gets a whiff of grouse, his head snaps up; he crouches and moves in the direction of the bird. In the parlance of the upland bird hunter; Mountie has gotten "birdy" and you know immediately when he is in that state. Ruffed grouse are great runners so he has to puzzle out the trail. He backtracks, moves forward nose to the ground following the scent trail. Meanwhile you have to keep up with the dog; all the while positioning yourself for a clear shot should the bird flush. If things work out, the bird flushes and a quick shot brings it down. Mountie has figured this upland bird thing out, and he knows instinctively where the bird has fallen. He moves in that direction, picks up the scent and brings the bird to hand. I am effusive in my praise, and we are both pleased as punch that the three-way dance between the bird, the hunter, and the dog has resulted in a bird in hand. I check the crop of the bird to see what it was eating; always instructive. And naturally I can hardly wait to get the bird in the oven; ruffed grouse are the finest of birds.

Mountie, however, is on his last legs. And it breaks our hearts to see him on the downward slope of his life. He stiffens up quickly, and I have to lift him bodily to get him onto the back seat of the truck. But the spirit is willing. Maybe I'll get a few hunts in with him this fall. I sure hope so.

ROBERT AND MOUNTIE WATERFOWL HUNTING
(On July 2, 2014, his body wracked with pain from the cancer and arthritis, Mountie was given that final injection by the veterinarian. He quietly closed his eyes for the last time with my arms around him and his family by his side. Rest easy old friend.)

On Choosing a Deer Rifle

(NOVEMBER 2004)

Small town coffee shops are great meeting places. The regulars gather at the same time every day during farming's off season and the friendly debates usually focus on some aspect of farming. From the best tractor, to the best breed of cattle, or to the attributes of today's crop of agriculture ministers, it's all fair game at coffee time.

And with the general deer season about to start, coffee shop debates have turned to the merits of various deer rifles. Deer are pursued in a wide range of habitats in Manitoba ranging from the wide open prairies of western Manitoba to the deep boreal forests of eastern Manitoba. This variety of hunting situations means that deer stalkers typically use a wide range of deer rifles depending on the areas they hunt and the type of hunting they do. Some hunters pursue all manner of big game and want a wide range of speciality rifles, one for each animal as it were, while others have that one rifle that does it all.

And for some, the choice of a rifle is as much based on sentiment and tradition as it is based on the performance of a specific calibre.

Ralph Smart farms near the western Manitoba town of Waskada and has chased whitetails for most of his life. Smart began hunting in the wide open areas and opted at that time for a "flat shooting" .270 calibre and 130 grain bullets. Over the years however, Smart changed his hunting style and spends most of his time deep in the woods waiting patiently on a trail for a deer to come by. He also uses "grunt calls" or "deer rattles" to lure bucks closer. His shots are now much closer and there are often some twigs between him and his prey.

Smart has settled on a bolt action .300 Winchester Short Magnum as his rifle of choice and uses a 180 grain bullet. Smart is quite technical and loads his own bullets and now gets the exact performance he wants.

"My .300 magnum shoots real well and won't be deflected by twigs. And since the .300 is big enough for moose, elk and caribou, this combination has become my all-around rifle," said Smart. "Besides, it's nice and light which makes it a pleasure to carry around."

Now while a 180 grain bullet seems heavy for deer, it's my bullet of choice as well. In the last few years I've gone back to my trusty .30-06 and it's quite accurate up to two hundred yards, far beyond where I shoot most of my deer anyway. I did try using some 150 grain bullets and was astonished at the difference in performance. So, since I hunt moose and elk as well and really didn't want to re-sight in my '06 every time I changed bullets, I've settled on this combination as my best deer rifle.

I have a friend who has only been hunting for three years but now lives for the deer season. Interestingly his deer rifle of choice is the versatile Thompson Centre Encore in a .30-06 calibre. The single-shot Encore is a relatively recent addition to the hunting scene and features interchangeable barrels and a "break open" action. With the advent of black powder hunting, single shot rifles seem to be making a comeback as hunters focus on making that first shot count.

Fellow fisheries biologist Shelley Matkowski chooses tradition over performance and hunts with her trusty pre-1969 era .30-30. Hers is a Model 94 Winchester lever action carbine, the rifle that is most often featured in those old westerns where the cowboys are rapidly firing from horseback. She disdains a scope and takes her deer at close range in the woods. As Matkowski puts it, "I've had so much fun with that little rifle."

Finally, there's Dick Gawiuk of Elphinstone who every now and then takes his 1904 vintage .38-55 out of the gun cabinet. Gawiuk describes this slow shooting rifle as "ballistically challenged." Still, he gets a real kick out of hunting with a hundred year old rifle.

"I like the old ways and even took a spike bull elk with that old gun a few years ago," he said.

I was awestruck by his description of that hunt when, on snowshoes in the deep woods, he managed to stalk the animal and take it with one shot.

Gawiuk, whose has hunted all over North America for a wide variety of game, says that regardless of the rifle there is no substitute for practise and really knowing where and how your gun shoots. "All that matters is where the bullet ends up," he noted. Amen to that.

ROBERT AND CAROLINE WITH A FALL BOUNTY OF VENISON AND FIREWOOD

Sighting In Your Big Game Rifle

(October 2008)

Manitoba's deer seasons are not that far off, and other big game seasons have already begun for some species. But no matter what game you pursue, "sighting in" your big bore rifle is a must. Sighting in makes sure that the rifle and its sights "agree" about where the bullet strikes.

Gravity operates the same way on an object whether it is moving or not. Thus a bullet starts to drop as soon as it leaves the rifle. Pointing a rifle up in the air, even slightly, means that the bullet would describe an arc since the upward angle of the muzzle would cause the bullet to fly up, but gravity would immediately start to pull the bullet back to earth. Remember this arc. Most big game hunters use telescopic sights so that's what we'll focus on.

Light is not affected by gravity, so the alignment of the scope on your rifle in relation to the barrel is important. The barrel is pointed ever so slightly upwards so the speeding bullet describes the arc discussed above and crosses the "line of sight" exactly twice; once near the shooter and once "way out there." This arc is the bullet's "trajectory." The highest distance between the line of sight and the bullet itself occurs halfway between the muzzle and where the bullet crosses the line of sight the second time. This is called the "mid-range trajectory." The attached diagram illustrates this.

For hunters who have just put scopes on their rifles the first step is to do a "bore sight." This means taking the action out of the rifle looking down the barrel at a close target, say ten yards. Then look through the scope and adjust it so the crosshairs are on the same target as the barrel or "bore." You are now in the ball park but far from being sighted in.

Sit in a chair with the rifle resting on a small table. Take three shots at twenty-five yards. If you are not exactly on target, adjust the scope until the rifle and scope agree that you are bang on at twenty-five yards. You've just established your first crossing point. A rough rule-of-thumb, after the twenty-five yard crossing point has been established, for most big game rifles with modern ammunition, is that you will be about three inches high at one hundred yards and bang on again at about two hundred and fifty yards, your second crossing point. You will want to take a few shots at a hundred yards to make sure. And make sure you use the same ammunition as you hunt with; different bullets perform differently.

I shoot the old reliable .30-06 with a 180 grain bullet. The ballistic chart tells me that this combination would be bang on at twenty-five yards, 2.8 inches high at one hundred yards and bang on again at two hundred and twenty-five yards. Visualize a bullet flying inside a long culvert the diameter of the "lethal" zone of the game you are after. In the case of white-tailed deer this is about eight inches. With a mid-range trajectory of 2.8 inches my .30-06 is well within that "culvert" and I can shoot with confidence at up to two hundred and twenty-five yards.

Practice putting your bullets where you want them to go. It's time well spent.

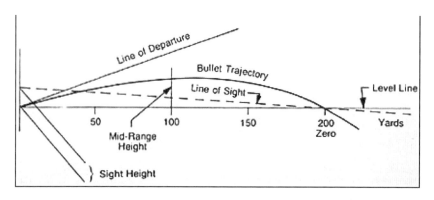

PARTS OF A TRAJECTORY

A Late Season Upland Bird Hunt

(December 2008)

"Sure, Bob. Come on down, and let's give those sharp-tails one last try," said Ralph Smart who farms near the town of Waskada. Smart, who also raises wild pheasants, also pointed out that there were a few "leftover" but very wily pheasants on his shooting preserve that we could try for. Sounded good.

I arrived at his neat farmstead early on the first day. It was fairly warm, but with the sweeping gale force winds that are common in that wide open Prairie landscape. There are two things you need to know about hunting late season sharp-tails. One, nobody else is crazy enough to be out there with you and, two, that late season sharp-tailed grouse are almost impossible to get.

I consider this Prairie grouse to be the perfect upland bird. They "hold" tight, fly well and let you get fairly close. But all of these "perfect" characteristics vanish by November. That's because late season birds tend to bunch up in large flocks and spend most of their time in the wide open. Getting within shotgun range is nearly impossible since there are dozens of pairs of eyes always on the lookout. One sign of danger and the flock vanishes.

But Smart and I were nothing if not determined and he knew a couple of brushy coulees where some birds might be holing up to get out of the wind. Sure enough as we drove down the prairie trail to one of those coulees a flock of birds arose but quickly settled down in the coulee. A real lucky break.

Smart knew exactly where the birds were, so we circled downwind and moved towards them. Helpers on this hunt were Smart's two German Wire-Hair Pointers; the ten-year-old veteran Sawyer and the exuberant youngster, two-year-old Rex. Moving up the draw, with Smart and I on the opposite slopes with Sawyer and Rex quartering back and forth in front of us, was akin to being in one of those "sporting art" paintings that express the choreography of an upland bird hunt. The diversity of native plant species and the soft hues of December just added to the magic.

And sure enough as we drew near to where we thought the birds were Smart nodded, and I moved quickly ahead. And just as the dogs got "birdy" the sharp-tails exploded from a hawthorn thicket. I managed to get one with my first shot but missed on the second.

With their big bodies and full feathering, late season sharp-tails are truly spectacular birds. We admired the plumage and the fully feathered "snowshoe" feet making it obvious that here was a bird well-adapted to whatever the harsh Prairie climate threw its way.

Smart, as befits his interest in hunting and farming, is a keen observer of nature.

"I see more sharp-tails now than I have seen in along time, and they seem to be on a steady increase."

Smart attributes this to the new farming system known as "zero-tillage," whereby this year's crop is sown into last year's stubble with very little disturbance creating safe and expansive "new" nesting grounds for sharp-tails. I'm inclined to agree with that hypothesis, and right then and there he and I decided to do some field investigations next spring to prove this out.

We hunted for the rest of the day and managed to pick up two more birds. An examination of their crops revealed a mixture of green leaves and buds. I suspect that buds will become more common as the snows pile up.

Of course one sees other wildlife while hunting, and the treat of the day for us was to flush ten mule deer. "Muleys," fairly rare in Manitoba, are a dramatic sight as they move over the open prairie landscape. Not only are they large but their distinctive jumping gait is unmistakable. Shortly after, we were treated to the sight of a young mule deer spike buck that almost walked up to us, "mule-sized" ears all twitching, as we crouched in the tall grass.

At the end of the day, we saw a flock of sharp-tails land right next to an old trail leading into an abandoned farmstead. *Gotcha,* we thought as we hatched a plot to sneak down the opposite sides of the trail and surprise the birds. Now the trick in this game is to exactly note where the birds are and come on them accordingly. Well, either we miscalculated or the birds ran to a different spot but when we charged over the trail we saw nothing but empty stubble. We had overestimated the distance.

Can't imagine how amused the birds must have been as they watched these two guys come charging over the trail, only to stand there looking foolish.

"We'll see you next year," laughed Smart as we watched the birds disappear over the horizon.

Caroline's favourite: Grouse a la King

Here is an adaptation from an old childhood favourite "chicken a la king", a great way to use sharp-tailed grouse. Sharp-tailed grouse have a more distinctive flavour than ruffed grouse and lends itself well to this recipe.

4 Sharp-Tailed Grouse (or Ruffies)
6 Tbsp butter
2 cups sliced mushrooms (if you are lucky and have some morels to mix with or use on their own—adds a wonderful flavour)
2 cups of frozen green peas
2 cups chicken broth
1 1/2 cups of milk or half and half
4-5 cups chopped grouse
Salt and pepper to taste
Paprika

Boil 4 sharp-tailed grouse in chicken broth for approximately 25 minutes. Remove grouse and retain broth for use later in the recipe. Remove grouse meat from the bone and chop into bite size pieces - set aside.

In large saucepan, melt butter. Stir in sliced mushrooms and cook until browned.

Add flour and whisk until blended. Slowly add the broth and the milk. Stir and bring to a boil and then reduce the heat until thickened.

Mix in chopped grouse and peas and continue cooking until meat and peas are heated through. Ladle onto toast and sprinkle with paprika.

Serves 6-8

A Hunting Day to Remember

(September 2002)

Sunday morning found me driving through beautiful Western Manitoba with Molly, my Chesapeake Bay Retriever, snoozing in pickup's back seat. We had arisen at five and the two-hour drive to the prairie country near the Saskatchewan border made me glad to be a hunter. Molly and I were going after that quintessential prairie bird, the sharp-tailed grouse.

It was a hunter's dawn in lonely country, but there were lessons to be learned every mile. Didn't see a vehicle for nearly the entire trip. I felt a bit lonely, but the loneliness was tempered by the abundance and grandeur of a fall prairie morning. The marshes were teeming with waterfowl, and in the eastern sky you could pick out the skeins of geese as they made their way to the fields. This was farm country, with all that implies, and the evidence of the fall harvest was everywhere. The juxtaposition of human hands on the landscape and the abundance of waterfowl showed that humans can use the earth while leaving some room for wildlife. The sun was so bright as it broke over the horizon that I had to dim the rear view mirror.

As I drove, I thought about the hunt we had on the Friday before with my two companions, Roland and Serge. I was the only one who had ever hunted sharp-tails, and they were eager to experience this bird that they had only read about. Friday was very windy. I knew from experience that this would change the birds' behaviour. They would normally feed in the open in the morning and then "retire" to the bluffs and shelterbelts for day. Hunting the bluffs late in the morning is usually rewarding.

On Friday, because of the wind, the sharp-tails stayed in the open. This may sound easy for the hunter but actually makes it more challenging since they can literally "see you coming." They were in flocks and, with many eyes watching, flushed wildly out of range as soon as they spied us. And when we did, in hunter's parlance, "mark them down" they would land in the open and again lead us on a merry chase. Over the course of the morning, we did each manage to get a few birds, which was all the more rewarding given the conditions.

In addition to the actual hunt, learning about the birds and bird habitat is also part of the process. A key question about any animal is "what are they feeding on?" This can give important clues about hunting strategies. Accordingly we inspected the "crops" of the birds during the bird cleaning process. The "crop" is the sac in the throat of a bird within which it stores food just before sending it for digestion. Interestingly, the crops of these sharp-tails held grasshoppers, sow-thistle flowers, and some alfalfa leaves. Made supreme sense especially when we saw the hordes of grasshoppers that exploded from the ground at nearly every step in the alfalfa fields where we found the birds. The adaptable sharp-tail is a hunter in its own right, and in my mind's eye I could just see them running through the fields pouncing on grasshoppers. The sow-thistle flowers were a revelation to me, never having seen them in the many sharp-tail crops that I have examined over the years. Food sources can change overnight as well, especially after the first killing frost. Frost puts an end to the grasshopper main course to be replaced by seeds, buds, and berries.

We ended off the day with a marvellous and entirely fortuitous duck hunt in a small wetland that had more water in it than I have ever seen in twenty-three years of hunting this country. Bodes well for next year's wetlands and waterfowl. Molly worked like a trooper all day, first on the grouse and then the ducks. She made one miraculous two hundred and fifty yard retrieve on a mallard that had us all applauding. Brought a lump into my throat actually since this will probably be her last hunting year. After eleven autumns, hundreds of hunts, and countless special moments it looks like she's coming to the end of the line. This year's hunts with her are all the more poignant.

Roland brought a fresh perspective to the day. He and his family left England over ten years ago to settle in western Manitoba. For him the day was simply, "over the moon," as the English would say. He noted that in England a day like this for the average person was simply not possible given the expanding human population and the extremely high cost of hunting. His reflections were not lost on Serge and I who, in our day jobs, work on wildlife and hunting issues. Ensuring that Manitoba's precious wildlife and hunting traditions are preserved will take much work but, as this day showed, it is well worth the effort.

A Wild Turkey at Last

(MAY 2008)

Ralph Smart was carefully working the turkey call, producing those seductive "hen tones" when we finally heard an answering gobble. And then another and another.

Maybe this *will be my time*, I thought to myself.

I felt quite lucky, especially after having won a brand new Stoeger over-and-under 12 gauge shotgun at the recent Delta Waterfowl dinner in Winnipeg. And, yes, feeling lucky is half the battle. After all, this was my fifth year of turkey hunting, and I had yet to provide my bride with a wild turkey for Thanksgiving. And her jibes were starting to hit a little too close to home!

I was out on the opening day of wild turkey season with the Smart clan, brothers Ralph and Owen and their dad, Franklin, all very experienced hunters. Ralph had scouted out a couple of farms and had obtained all of the necessary permissions. Wild turkeys are not native to Manitoba, having been introduced to the Keystone Province in the 1950s. The bird has developed a unique symbiosis with farmers and ranchers by utilizing cattle feedlots and the woods surrounding them as over-wintering areas. But as spring turns to summer the birds disperse throughout the countryside.

We met early in the morning near the hunting spot and split up with Ralph and I going south and Owen and Franklin hunting north but near the farmstead. It must be emphasized though, that just because wild turkeys "hang around" with people, they are far from being pushovers when it comes to hunting. A non-hunter could be forgiven for thinking that chasing farm country turkeys is nothing more than, well, a "turkey shoot."

Boy, nothing could be farther from the truth. Every predator from hawks and owls to foxes and coyotes wants a turkey dinner, and the bird's legendary wariness, bolstered by unbelievably keen eyesight, makes them a challenging quarry.

We were all using turkey decoys; usually one hen and one tom. The theory is that you attract a male bird by the call, who then sees the about-to-be-mating pair, and comes a'running to fight off the male and grab the female for himself. That's the theory anyway. Ralph and I heard no birds but could hear toms calling further north towards Franklin and Owen, so we pulled up stakes and moseyed on over. They had had a group of birds in front of them but for one reason or another were unable to take one.

"We saw them move down the trail," said Owen. "They weren't too spooked and maybe we can set up the decoys and call one in."

We readily agreed, and the rest was history. Having a big tom turkey move towards your calling spot is one of the most exciting hunting experiences. You track the bird's progress by the call and hope against hope that nothing goes wrong. In this case it played out perfectly for Ralph and me. He played that "come hither" tune on the call, and I waited with breathless anticipation as the bird moved warily towards us. Finally his head and neck appeared just by some deadfall along the trail some twenty metres away.

This is it, I thought.

I clicked off the safety, aimed at a spot at the base of the head, pulled the trigger and down he went. My five-year turkey drought was over, and our Thanksgiving dinner was secured.

Caroline's favourite:
Roast Wild Turkey in a Baking Bag

> Wild turkey has a wonderful rich flavour and we love the gravy from it. It is really important not to overcook the turkey. Unlike domestic turkey, all of the meat is dark and it is lean. If you do not have a baking bag, follow the same recipe but be careful not to overcook.
>
> Preheat oven to 325 degrees.

1 wild turkey (5 to 10 lbs)

Rub bird with salt and pepper.

Stuffing options:

Use your favourite bread stuffing or insert: quartered apples, quartered medium onion and 4 ribs of celery chopped.

Insert meat thermometer into the centre of the thigh.

Put the wild turkey into the roasting bag and tie the bag closed. Roast until thermometer reads 165°F and juices are just slightly pink from the thigh.

Unstuffed bird - roast for approximately 10-12 minutes per pound.

Stuffed bird - roast for approximately 12-14 minutes per pound.

Remove turkey from oven and let stand for 25 minutes before removing from bag.

For gravy, pour the juice from the bag into a saucepan. Mix together a paste of flour and water. Whisk into juices and bring to a boil being sure to whisk constantly. If using the apples as stuffing the juices and pulp from the apple add a nice flavour to the gravy. If gravy is too thick add and stir in chicken broth.

Robert and His First Wild Turkey

Lessons Learned on the Hunting Trails

(December 2009)

One year I was fortunate to have been drawn for a Landowner elk/moose tag south of Riding Mountain National Park where our land is located. Manitoba Conservation has restricted the number of these licenses (much to the consternation of local landowners) so it was as if I'd won a lottery. And in a manner of speaking I had, since the extended Landowner season takes up much of the fall plus a week in mid-December and one in late December. Sounds easy, doesn't it? And I cannot tell you how often I get asked the question, "got your elk tied up yet?" The implication being, of course, that having this tag automatically means meat in the freezer. Well, Mother Nature is usually not that accommodating and sure enough here I am at the end of my time in the landowner season, elk-less and moose-less (rhymes with useless, but I digress).

Anyway, I had great fun trudging up and down my hills, across the meadows, and through the bogs searching for those elusive creatures. Early on I'd make moose calls and elk bugles and sometimes come across tracks. Once I heard a great crashing through the bush and surmised that I'd flushed a moose. I never get too "fussed" about this venture, though. The autumn's bird hunting had been going splendidly, and I was pretty sure about getting a deer, so having wild meat in our freezer was not really the issue. Still and all I kept hunting. So it was with boundless optimism that I returned home on December 16 from a work stint in Alberta, hoping to take in the last few days of the landowner season. There was enough tracking snow and I figured the cold spell had caused animals to move in although one of my neighbours said, "Bob, we're sure not seeing too many."

Well, as they say, "hope springs eternal" so I walked my hills for three days last week but saw nary an animal. But it's a funny thing about hunting. The anticipation of an animal keeps you going… and going… and going. Hunting is not like going for a walk although in my case the outcomes were the same. This may be hard for a non-hunter to understand, but the Spanish philosopher Ortega y Gasset in his seminal book *Meditations on Hunting* described a hunter as "The Alert Man." The prospect of seeing an animal, the subsequent stalk, the ensuing shot, and maybe the tragedy/triumph of the kill bestow a keenness on the experience, no matter how fruitless the outcome. The air is fresher, the scenery is more dramatic, and the anticipation more pronounced; even, as in my case, if you've walked the same land for decades.

I saw more ruffed grouse sign that I expected and, on two occasions, was startled into breathlessness by the explosive flush of these speedsters. I saw where a fisher had been searching for his dinner and noted that snowshoe hare numbers seemed to be increasing, if their tracks were any indication. And I came across some really big deer tracks; no doubt from those elusive "hill bucks" that we rarely, if ever, encounter. And the crowning glory was to come upon a fresh den with a halo of frost around the opening. It was for certain a bear; no doubt enjoying a long, and hopefully uninterrupted, hibernation until spring.

Did I get my elk or moose? No, I didn't. Was it a successful hunt? You bet it was.

Your Eyes in the Woods

(August 2009)

When it comes to hunting and angling I try to minimize my use of electronic technology. After all, I have a firearm and/or modern angling equipment, which my quarry does not have, so in the interests of fairness I "should" go out there as "bare bones" as I can. But every now and then a technology comes along that delivers such interesting results that it becomes nigh on irresistible. Such as it was for me with trail cameras, or "trail cams" as they are most often referred to.

Hunters and naturalists are always trying to figure out the movements of wildlife and/or the size and gender of an animal in question. On my own trails I'd often see elk, moose or deer tracks which poses the usual set of questions. "When did it walk by?" "How big is it?" "Will there be others along shortly?" And since few have the requisite time or patience to sit quietly in the woods for hours on end, many of us have opted to set up "trail cams" at special spots hoping to get a photo of the animal, or animals, in question.

Trail cams are simply battery operated cameras with motion detectors. An animal comes into view, and a photo is taken. A time and date stamp is affixed to the photo so you know exactly when said animal walked by your setup. My own trail cams are inexpensive (less than $200) and are set to take a shot every fifteen seconds when there is motion in the field of view. I set mine up at feeding areas and choke points and the results have far exceeded my expectations.

Bull Elk Taken with Trail Cam

Quite literally, trail cams open up a whole new world of wildlife viewing possibilities. In my case, I had no idea of the wildlife activity on my land. At one of my spots this year and last, I photographed a magnificent bull elk both in velvet and after he had worn the velvet off. There were also two elk cows with calves plus a nice doe whitetail with a new fawn of her own. The beauty of the date and time stamp is that after enough "hits" you will be able to pattern a specific animal and develop your hunting plan accordingly.

Other wildlife that I have taken with a trail cam are snowshoe hares, red fox, lynx, raccoon and coyotes.

One problem, however, that I had NOT anticipated was bears. I had set up the trail cam at a likely spot full of elk tracks and was eager to see what I had "caught" after first full week. Just as an aside, the eager anticipation of checking a trail cam is just like checking a trapline; you repeatedly ask the question, "What did I get?" Well, when I got to the site, the trail cam had been torn off the tree and was lying in a pile of leaves looking up taking pictures of the swaying treetops. Good grief! It didn't take long to point the finger at an inquisitive black bear whose nose filled the entire frame of one photograph, presumably just before he tore it down. Firstly I thought this was a one off occurrence, but after it happened a few times it became apparent that I had a problem. I tried cayenne pepper sprinkled on the tree, but that didn't work. I basically had to live with it until the bears went into hibernation. But, y'know, we really like bear sausage at our house, and the spring season will soon be upon us. So maybe I CAN fix this problem.

Hunting Whitetails in the Big Woods of the Boreal Forest

(October 2007)

Five years ago I lost a deer hunting partner: my brother, Tim.

He didn't pass away, and no tragedy befell him. Rather, after twenty years of hunting with me in western Manitoba's farm country, he relocated to the woods, rocks and swamps of the Whiteshell Provincial Park in southeastern Manitoba.

The other day I asked him why he switched. "You mean, other than your bad jokes and god-awful lunches?" he quipped.

His son, Mark, was just starting to hunt deer, and Tim decided that the open country, walk-and-stalk hunting that we favoured didn't work well for a beginner. And with a family cottage in the Whiteshell, where deer numbers were healthy, it seemed like the perfect opportunity to try hunting from stands along game trails.

Tim recommends that first-timers in the "big woods" focus on hunting from blinds. "This reduces your chances of getting lost and creates quality shooting opportunities," he explained.

Tim only hunts from ground blinds. He sets in four corner posts using five-centimetre-diameter sticks and lashes on cross-pieces that are set at about waist height and double as shooting rests. He then uses a hatchet and light machete to clear shooting lanes. The whole process takes a couple of hours, and is done long before the hunting season. When hunting, he hangs camouflage netting around the blind and brings along a bucket or folding stool to sit on. "I often have two blinds in good locations and settle in according to the wind," said Tim.

Not to mention the additional risks, Tim tells me tree stands are unnecessary if you pick your locations well. Having grown up with the guy, I'm convinced his legendary frugality keeps him from buying one! However, he continues to shoot nice bucks, all from ground blinds.

The next piece of advice is to stay put. My friend, Herb Goulden, former provincial Deer Manager and seasoned Turtle Mountains hunter, says that forest deer move throughout the day. Tim agrees. "While 9:00 am to 11:00 am has been my best window, I've taken animals through the day. Dress for the elements, arrive at first light and stick around. On cold days I'll take breaks to move off stand, build a fire and make tea."

To his normal packsack items—matches, knife, compass, first aid, hot liquids, snacks, emergency blanket, flashlight and extra clothes—Tim adds a GPS unit. "This gives me the peace of mind to set up off the beaten track," he said. "There's comfort in having your vehicle or boat marked when you're a mile away on a cloudy day."

Experienced Whiteshell hunters advised him to find choke points that funnel animal movements. Animal densities are lower, overall, so it's especially important to locate the high percentage spots.

"We focused on waterways that were heavily dammed by beavers," said Tim. "Air photos were invaluable, but we also took many walks in the woods."

Spots that looked good on air photos sometimes turned out to be duds, but a few gems revealed themselves. "I'm now getting a sense of the mixes of habitat that will hold deer and, as important, the landscape features that concentrate their movements," said Tim.

Much has been written about rattling and calls. Tim uses both and has taken at least three bucks that responded to rattling. He generally rattles no more than every thirty minutes.

Hunting in farm country is easier than how Tim hunts the forest, but he's hooked on the Canadian Shield's beauty and solitude. Many species of birds are still migrating through, and there's the chance for encounters with bigger woodland denizens. "One day my son and I were surrounded by two groups of howling wolves. Boy, did that get the deer moving, not to mention the hair on my neck!" said Tim.

And as for the old saw that "bush deer" are about as tasty as swamp grass, Tim has a simple answer: "Hogwash. We've taken thirteen animals, many were bucks more than two years old, and they've all been great eating. I'll put my forest deer steaks up against farmland deer any time."

He still remembers their first hunt vividly. They planned it for the end of the muzzleloader season and the opening of the general season to coincide with school holidays. But Mother Nature threw a curve.

"It snowed that week and then, the day before leaving, a brutal cold spell set in. It dropped to −20°C," said Tim. "What a way to begin our experiment, especially for a fourteen-year-old who was on the runty side in those days!"

With the arrival of snow and cold, some of their best-looking spots were suddenly abandoned. After two fruitless days on stand in frigid cold, Mark was losing heart. That evening the weather broke and temperatures nudged at the freezing point. Mark managed to find a little hope.

The day dawned clear and calm, but warm. They crept to their stand at first light and, by the pour of their first cup of tea, a nice buck appeared on the edge of their beaver flood. Mark lay his .308 on the blind's shooting rest, took a deep breath, slowly exhaled and squeezed the trigger.

Mark's aim was true and the deer was down quickly. And, as the vagaries of hunting sometimes play out, Mark filled their second tag on a nice young buck from the same stand four hours later.

From that beginning, they've taken Whiteshell white-tails every season, including some impressive bucks. "The challenges and joys of hunting in the Canadian Shield have completely changed my outlook," said Tim. "Now, I'm just not all that interested in hunting anywhere else," he said.

Sounds like I've lost my deer hunting partner for good, unless I gas up the truck and head east!

Today the Elk Won

(February 2003)

Well, I said to myself, *time to shut down the computer and go for an elk walk, because you just never know.* Monday January 27 was the opening day of the extended elk seasons around Riding Mountain National Park. I knew that the cold weather would cause the elk to move about more as their food requirements increased.

It was a strong west wind, which meant that I had to first circle south around where I thought any elk might be, move to the eastern boundary of my land, and then slowly hunt back west against the wind. Today the wind was my friend as it not only blew my scent away from the elk but the sound of the wind in the trees would mask the sounds of me crunching through the snow.

Still and all, the elk have the advantage, especially in the rough, hilly terrain that they, and I too for that matter, call home. There's something about hunting that makes the event much more than a mere walk in the woods. Even if the odds are slim, you are on edge and alert.

On the south end of one of my lakes, I saw those heart-stopping signs in the snow; fresh elk tracks and there were two sets of them! All of a sudden my odds just got a whole lot better. Now I know my hundred and sixty acres like the back of my hand, but then again so do the animals. *Now what*, I asked myself. Blundering after the animals by following the tracks was hopeless so I circled ahead, hoping to cut them off. I moved along one of my trails but soon noted that they were cutting east so I backtracked almost to where I first saw the tracks and tried to encircle them again, all the time walking in such a direction that my scent would be blown away from the animals.

I stood on a point overlooking a small lake and could see fresh tracks crossing the lake further along. *Rats*, I thought, *they've crossed the lake and moved further east into the big woods. I'll never get a chance now.*

But, one of the lessons I've learned about hunting is that you always finish the hunt because you just never know. Well as I moved up the next hill it happened. There across the lake in a thicket was an animal. I upped the scope and sure enough, a nice cow elk. Trouble was she was in thick brush, so I needed to get closer to even hope for a clear shot. I backtracked, crossed the lake and slipped silently along the shore using the bank as cover. Sure enough, there she was but in too much brush to shoot. So I scrambled up the bank hoping to get a better view plus to use the trees as a rest to shoot from.

The elk was still there, about seventy-five yards away but behind a screen of willows and poplar trees. The wind was good so here I sat, peering through the scope, squinting, and searching, hoping for a shot. I had the safety on and off about five times as she moved around but never presenting me with a good shooting opportunity. I was determined to wait for a clear chance. The thought of wounding the animal was more than I could bear.

As experienced hunters can appreciate, after ten minutes of this I was starting to get a little frantic especially since I knew that the hills were capable of deflecting my scent towards the elk. *I better try to get a clear shot*, I thought. *Or it's all over.* I was hoping that the still strong wind would cover any noise I might make. And if I could not see the elk, then it could not see me, or so I figured. I moved closer, almost swimming through the thigh deep snow. But when I got near to where the elk had been, it was gone. I didn't see it go nor did I hear it; she just vanished. As I stood there dejectedly I could only marvel at how close I had come. The elk had won.

As I took that long walk home, I kept replaying the experience and second-guessing myself. By the time I got home I concluded that I'd done everything right and that this outcome was simply meant to be. And I said to myself, *There's always another day.*

So what are the lessons of a hunt like this? Number one: The best time to go hunting is whenever you can. Number two: Hunt hard and never give up. Number three: Wait for the good shots even if it means coming home empty-handed. Number four: The ultimate benefit of hunting is the great stories you get. And I just bagged one.

Paralyzed by Elk

(PREVIOUSLY UNPUBLISHED)

Elk are among the most magnificent big game animals in North America. Celebrated by hunters and non-hunters alike, the elk is the only animal to have the appellation "Royal" applied to it since the biggest elk are called "royal bulls." The animal even has a large service club, "The Elks," named after it!

I shot my first elk in 1984. It was fairly easy; a cow came out of the woods to my alfalfa field and one shot was all it took. But that was it for easy elk.

My second elk was a much more challenging affair. Jonathan Scarth, my late friend Mike Bessey and I were hunting elk on the East side of Riding Mountain National Park. We were at our posts early and just as legal shooting time came I heard that distinctive sound of willow twigs snapping on antlers. A big elk was coming my way! It came in range, I upped my rifle, shot, and then off he ran. I wasn't worried; I was sure that I made a good shot. Turns out I didn't. I had hit him too far back. Too make a long story short we followed a blood trail for over two kilometres. We finally caught up to the elk, dispatched him and then spent until the late evening hauling this big animal out. My friend Mike, after the six hour drag was nearly over, was moved to note in a weary voice, "If this is male bonding, how come I hate you guys." Mike's quote brought much-needed levity to our weary hunting troop. This elk proved what many hunters know; the stamina of elk is legendary.

But from that point on I have been paralyzed by elk. What I mean by the term "paralyzed" is that from that point on I have frozen up when I have had the chance to shoot an elk. I think that the experience with the wounded elk had traumatized me so much that I was always waiting for that perfect shot.

I remember a cow elk that I surprised on my land during one landowner elk season about ten years ago. I turned the corner on a path, and there she was. But when I brought my rifle up I just stopped for a nano-second. And that is all any elk needs. She wheeled around and was gone in a flash. *Why didn't you shoot?* I kept asking myself on the long trudge home.

And just two years ago, again on my own land during the special landowner season, I was driving home and right across my farm road I saw a mass of elk tracks heading into my woods. Naturally I quickly got my hunting gear and went after them. I didn't follow the tracks directly but moved to cut them off and moved to circle round and head them off. Wonder of wonders, it worked! I flushed one cow who was off before I could shoot, but when I came over the hill, I saw five more plus a real nice bull standing on the ice on one of my small ponds. He was in a perfect spot but I kept moving to get that perfect shot. Turns out I waited too long and with a quick move they all wheeled away. Again, and to this day, I think about that experience. *Why didn't I shoot?* All I could say was that I was paralyzed by elk. Maybe some year I'll get over it.

The White-Tailed Deer's Fall Drama

(November 2005)

Recently, the Manitoba Public Insurance Corporation (MPIC) has been warning motorists about the increasing dangers of car accidents involving white-tailed deer. Costing Manitoba motorists millions of dollars annually, these collisions reach a peak in the fall due to the increasing activity levels of deer.

White-tailed deer mate in the fall, a process known as the rut. The rut is not just a one-time breeding event but is a whole chain of events leading up to the actual mating."

One Manitoban who has probably logged more time watching and hunting white-tails is the Fort Whyte Centre's Site Manager, Ken Cudmore. He has observed Fort Whyte's white-tails for decades and has developed a keen sense of what makes this wonderful animal "tick." He's also in the woods every fall with his bow, sitting in his tree stand watching, waiting, and hunting deer.

"The mating process actually starts when male whitetails begin to form antlers," Cudmore explained. "This and all subsequent rutting activities are governed by day length, or photoperiod. As day length decreases, change happens on almost a daily basis; it's really a remarkable time.

"In August a buck's antlers are still in the fragile velvet stage. And bucks are "hanging around" in bachelor groups," he noted. "In early September the velvet is shed, usually in one day, and by late September the bachelor groups begin to disintegrate and the bucks become solitary. As the day length decreases, by mid-October the bucks begin "working out," that is they start to tear apart shrubs and small trees. This builds their strength for the battles ahead.

"Then the bucks become more aggressive to other bucks and by late October really don't tolerate each other's company. Their "workouts" have made them stronger and their necks start to swell due to the rising levels of testosterone."

Cudmore noted that at this point, a buck will deposit scent from a gland on his forehead on small trees at so-called "signal rubs." This tells other bucks that "this is my land."

"It's then that the bucks really begin to take an interest in the does and, in late October or early November, start to make "scrapes." A scrape is made when a buck uses his front hooves to clear a small patch of ground of all leaves and debris," he explained. "Scrapes are always under overhanging branches upon which he deposits another smell signal, this time from scent glands located under his eyes. He also chews on the branches. Finally he urinates down his leg and onto the scrape, the urine picking up yet another smell signal from glands located on his leg. All of this tells a doe that this buck is here and ready."

By mid-November the rut is in full swing. Bucks visit their scrapes on a daily basis to see if a doe had been by. Cudmore explained that when a doe is in heat she will visit a scrape, lick the same branches that the buck scented, and then urinate in the scrape. This causes the buck to go looking for the doe and mating ensues.

Bucks will fight each other for the rights to breed. Small bucks will spar with other small bucks but that is a far cry from the "knock-'em-down-drag-'em-out" fights between monster bucks.

"Most mature bucks don't fight since they can bluff away smaller bucks, but when two bucks of equal size meet, look out," explained Cudmore. "I saw one fight where a big buck was confronted by a bigger challenger who proceeded to flip the first buck right on its back. The challenger then calmly walked away with the first buck's doe."

The rut is an ideal time to hunt big buck deer. Not only are they less wary, but the rut opens up a whole new repertoire of hunting techniques especially "rattling." Rattling involves the hunter clashing together a set of antlers to simulate a fight between two bucks.

"Rattling is simply the very best way to hunt," said Cudmore. "Rattling will draw bucks from a long way thinking that other bucks have invaded their territory or that a receptive doe is being fought over and maybe he'll have a chance to mate."

And when it comes to Ken Cudmore and big bucks the proof is in the pudding, but to Cudmore hunting is more than the kill.

"Hunting is not so much about the actual kill, although I do love putting a healthy supply of meat in my family's freezer. My most memorable hunting days have been ones when I never fired an arrow. I think I've learned more about nature in one afternoon sitting in a tree than I did in an entire semester of university."

I certainly agree.

November Buck at Early Morning

The Ruffed Grouse—A Manitoba Treasure

(October 2002)

Most hunters have their favourite species, and for me it has to be the ruffed grouse, sometimes referred to as the "drummer of the woods." The ruffed grouse was my first quarry as a young hunter, and it is with great fondness that I recall those early days. Brother Tim and I would trail after Dad searching the thickets of the boreal forest for ruffed grouse. When we did get a bird, the big fight was over who got to carry it!

The ruffed grouse is uniquely North American. Stretching from Alaska to Newfoundland and south to Virginia, the ruffed grouse is one of our most widely distributed upland birds. No wide open prairies for this bird, it is a true forest grouse and its distribution almost exactly follows the distribution of the aspen tree. No other plant provides ruffed grouse with the quality of cover and food resources. A common sight in the parkland is a ruffed grouse "budding" in an aspen tree silhouetted against the evening sky. Their prime winter food are the buds of the trembling aspen, but interestingly it is the highly nutritious male aspen buds that are most utilized.

The ruffed grouse is the most beloved of all upland birds. Poems, books, and innumerable scientific studies have tried to describe the grace, beauty, and ecology of this superbly adapted bird and its various names reflect this attention. According to the 1947 landmark study entitled "The Ruffed Grouse—Life History, Propagation and Management," this bird has no less than thirty-seven English names and twenty-two names in other languages. Locally the ruffed grouse is mistakenly referred to as a "partridge," a name more properly applied to other upland birds. In Quebec the ruffed grouse is called *"la gelinot hupee."* "Pat," "willow grouse," "ruffie," and "wood pheasant" are some of its other names while the Chippewas called it *"wen gi-da-bi-ne."* There's even "The Ruffed Grouse Society" based in Coraopolis, Pennsylvania.

I live in the middle of prime ruffed grouse habitat, and the relationship we have with the bird is both profound and uplifting. Spring is here when the first ruffed grouse drumming echoes through the woods. Grouse drumming sounds like a motorcycle in the distance revving and fading, and the sound is so low you "feel" it as much as hear it. Male grouse drum by anchoring themselves to a fallen log and then beating their wings for all they are worth to attract a female.

Females lay between nine and fourteen eggs, and the chicks hatch out to a life of peril. Seems like everything wants to eat ruffed grouse. Ruffed grouse populations rise and crash with great regularity. Right now ruffed grouse are increasing in the western parkland area of Manitoba and are scarce in the east and south. This will no doubt change over the next few years.

An endearing feature is that ruffed grouse respond barely if at all to human intervention. It cannot be raised, stocked, or managed to any degree, and the populations wax and wane in a manner completely indifferent to humanity. On our land all I can do is make trails, create forest openings, and plant clover. Ruffed grouse need "young forests" and, like many "early successional species" such as white-tailed deer, are helped by modern forestry.

In the North woods, late October and after is the time to be out hunting ruffed grouse. The leaves are gone and the bird is much easier to find, plus many regions are experiencing a grouse resurgence. I just love to hunt ruffies with Molly, my big Chesapeake Bay retriever. Over the years we've become real partners, enhanced by her great experience with the bird. She, in effect, leads me through the woods searching out grouse in prime habitat. And if I get a bird, I always check its "crop" or food sac at the base of its throat. You can learn a lot about the bird's habits by examining what foods it had just consumed. I plant my trails to legumes like alfalfa, a favourite food, and get really "jazzed" when I see "my" alfalfa in a bird's crop.

Yesterday we had marvellous late afternoon hunt on some agricultural Crown land that has the right mix of fields, thickets, food, and trails. We flushed over ten birds in two hours and came home with four. It was the misses that I'll remember, one in particular. Molly was acting real "birdy," that is sending out the body language saying she was in the middle of hot bird scent. I was so intent on her that I missed the grouse that flushed from a bush at eye level not two metres away. The booming flush rattled me so much that I flubbed an easy "going away" shot. Grouse often wait until you are right upon them before they flush, and by the time you regain your composure they are gone. A booming ruffed grouse flush has got to rank right up there as one of the most dramatic hunting experiences.

Soon it will be winter, but the ruffed grouse are ready for that. With their "snowshoe" feet that allow them to float over deep snow and their propensity to dig little snow caves for protection, they are ready for anything. Asking nothing and taking nothing, the ruffed grouse will be drumming long after we are gone. One author summed it up by saying:

"To know the grouse is to love it; And loving it, to wish it well." Amen.

Contents from a Ruffed Grouse Crop

Being in the Woods Has Its Own Rewards

(June 2008)

One of the great rewards of being a hunter and living life in the natural world are the unbelievable sights you see. And while not disparaging other form of outdoor recreation, a person's senses become ultra keen when hunting.

Ralph Smart from Waskada, Manitoba, is one of those alert hunters who had a most extraordinary experience while bear hunting this spring. In his own words:

"I was in my tree stand overlooking the bear bait in anticipation of a big black bear moving in. There was lots of activity in the area, and I was pretty hopeful. Suddenly, a movement caught my eye. I looked closely down the trail that I had just come in on and to my amazement a fisher stepped into the opening."

Fishers are members of the weasel family but weigh between two and seven kilograms so are quite large for a weasel. Fishers are becoming more common and are very agile predators as Smart will attest to.

"I knew that fishers were hard to spot so I stayed still to enjoy this sight. Suddenly the fisher looked back as if real nervous and I soon saw why," Smart continued. "Coming up the same trail, hot on the fisher's tracks, was a small black bear. The bear ran at the fisher who immediately climbed up a poplar tree. The bear climbed after the fisher and pretty soon both animals were in the treetops swaying in the breeze. The fisher turned towards the bear, snapping and hissing and the bear growled right back. It didn't take long for the fisher to say "I'm outta here" and he jumped to a nearby tree and then to another that he climbed down and then took off like a scalded cat. I have never, ever seen anything like it!"

But the story wasn't over and Smart continued: "The bear was way too small for me to shoot," Smart explained. "And I was happy just to watch the show. The bear slowly climbed down the tree, strolled over to the bait and proceeded to chow down. After a few mouthfuls, he decided to check my tree out. I wasn't sure he knew what I was, but he moved to the base of my tree and then looked right at me. I didn't move, but once he looked away I got out my camera and started taking pictures. This bear didn't have a care in the world, and after playing around at the base of my tree decided to stretch out right below me. He looked pretty content, and I bet if there was a hammock there he would have climbed into it!"

At this point things turned even more interesting, Smart recalled, "Just as the "teenager" was settling in for his nap, with me wondering how I was going to deal with this, the small bear snapped to attention and stared down the same trail. At that point a much bigger adult bear strolled into view and made threatening sounds towards the smaller animal. The "teenager" knew right away that his time was up and he high-tailed it through the bush. It's amazing what you see when you are hunting!

Nature in Action

(February 2004)

We hunters are offered ringside seats to some of Nature's most awesome spectacles. Waterfowl hunters thrill to skeins of ducks and geese from horizon to horizon, wild turkey hunters get to call their quarry within metres of their blinds, and elk hunters can thrill to the answering bugle of an angry bull.

Hunters often witness the life and death struggles that make nature "red in tooth and claw" as described by Jack London. And I have been especially fortunate in this regard.

A few years ago, I was deer hunting in early November during the black powder season with my dear friend Mike Bessey, who tragically passed away at far too young an age. We were slowly walking through a wooded pasture about fifty metres apart. Wooded pastures usually lack underbrush which makes for good visibility. As I moved along, I could hear the sounds of very excited magpies. As I reached a little clearing I could see them dive bombing something in a little willow thicket.

Now the snow was late that year, and snowshoe hare numbers were high. Hares turn white in the late fall, but we had the situation where the hares were white but there was no snow. This allowed us to easily spot the white creatures on the brown forest floor. As I peered into the willows I could see a white object bouncing around on the forest floor.

I knew that it was a hare and surmised that it had been the victim of a predator attack and that it had escaped. The magpies, obviously, were trying to dispatch the wounded creature and attain an easy meal. The hare bounced into view, and I could see a broken leg flopping around as the hare desperately tried to reach cover. Well, I *thought* it was a leg.

I hadn't moved a muscle up to this point. When the hare finally stopped I counted five appendages and realized that what I thought was a flopping front leg was really a white weasel with its razor-sharp teeth firmly locked in a death grip at the throat of the hare. I could see the flashing eyes of the hare and felt the grim determination of the weasel to hang on. The hare was easily four to five times as big as the weasel, and when the hare started to gyrate around, it was all that the weasel could do to maintain its grip. But it did. And every time the exhausted hare stopped, I could see the weasel take an even firmer grip, sinking its fangs deeper into the throat of the hare. Eventually the hare succumbed and quietly died. The weasel kept hold, as if reluctant to take a chance with such a hard one prize. Finally I moved and the weasel looked up and straight at me, its red, bloody mouth in stark contrast to its snow white fur. There was no fear, only the unspoken message—*this hare is mine*. Naturally, I acquiesced and moved on, marvelling at what I had just witnessed.

Another time I was taking an early spring walk in our woods when I saw a yearling deer on the shores of one of the many small lakes in this area. It was quartering away from me, obviously intent on something. I waited. A coyote came into view and faced the little deer; a classic Mexican standoff. The coyote wanted the deer and moved ahead. But instead of running, the young deer stamped its feet and charged the predator which promptly swapped ends and ran. The deer stopped. The coyote stopped. The deer started to move away and the coyote came at the deer again. The deer turned, stamped its feet, and charged the coyote. Same result. After a few more times the coyote knew that this was one meal that it was not going to get and melted away, as did the deer. I have always respected white-tails, but I had not appreciated their fighting ability.

We often see the predatory birds known as Northern Harriers (formerly called marsh hawks) when we're duck hunting. Two years ago, while hunting on a point, we shot a blue winged teal that landed on the shore opposite the point. I put the dog in the boat and proceeded to row across to the other side thinking that we'd have a tough time finding it. I needn't have worried since just then a harrier swooped down where the duck was, grabbed it, and tried to lift off. Now harriers are not that big, and this one simply could not lift the sodden duck. It sat on its prize until I hove into view, sighed in frustration (well, I imagined it sighed), and abandoned the duck.

These are but a few of the wonders of nature that hunters experience.

Rattling for Big Bucks Works for Veteran Hunter

(October 2009)

Waskada, Manitoba native Ralph Smart has been deer hunting for thirty of his forty-five years and has basically "seen it all." But unlike most deer hunters, who usually begin as rifle hunters, he started out as a bow-hunter.

"I spent a lot of time in trees stands where the deer were completely oblivious to my presence," recalled Smart. "And I was able to observe a lot of fascinating deer behaviour up close and personal, as it were."

Smart's most thrilling observations related to the two times when he was able to observe big bucks fighting for dominance with the ultimate prize being the right to breed a receptive doe.

Buck deer grow antlers for a reason. Antlers are related to establishing dominance over inferior bucks and ultimately passing on superior genes to the next generation. Antlers are what biologists call "secondary sexual characteristics" and, apparently, large antlers size and big physical bucks equate to superior survival characteristics. Big bucks get big for a reason; they are smart, secretive, and adept at eluding predators, including humans. But when it comes to the October–November rutting season, big bucks tend to "lose it" in their intense urge to breed. Some interesting human parallels here that we don't need to go into! And hunters have learned to take advantage of this weakness by "rattling" for deer.

"I was able to observe the sequence of events that took place during the buck fights I witnessed," said Smart. "The two bucks would circle each other and display by holding their ears back like aggressive dogs and tilt their heads; they looked like a pair of boxers circling each other. They then got close, forcefully locked horns and began to really push, shove, and grunt."

Smart noted that, "On both occasions the noise of the fight brought in other deer. The clashing of a set of antlers will bring in other bucks who are hoping to "cash in" on a receptive doe.

Smart described his rattling process:

"I move into the wind and find a spot in the woods but where I can see about a hundred metres. I pick a spot by a deadfall. Once I'm set up, I stamp the ground, start breaking branches to give the impression of mayhem. I give three or four loud grunts with my deer call. I then take a set of antlers and crash them together forcefully and then twist them together back and forth for about a minute or until my arms get too tired. This sounds like two deer locked together in mortal combat."

Smart advises the "rattler" to be at maximum alertness since an excited buck can come in very quickly. He strongly recommends the use of a "safari sling" that holds the rifle at the horizontal about waist height. In this way the hunter can drop the antlers and the rifle will be readily accessible.

"My most memorable rattling experience was one where I didn't even get the deer," Smart recounted. "I had rattled for about thirty seconds when I saw a deer looking at me in thick brush from ten metres away. I saw small tines and assumed it was a small spike buck. But when I moved he lifted his head and all I saw was the backside of a huge six by six buck hightailing it out of there."

Smart went on to note that has taken twelve nice bucks using the rattling technique and three of them are in the Boone and Crockett record book. Try rattling; you just might take that monster!

The Joys of Late Season Ruffed Grouse Hunting

(December 2008)

My big Chesapeake Bay Retriever, Mountie, approached the "Berry Covert," as we call a certain thick stand of chokecherries, and I could see he was getting "birdy." Getting "birdy" is the term hunters use to describe the behaviour of their dogs when they detect the hot scent of a nearby upland bird. In this case we were after ruffed grouse, which many Manitobans mistakenly refer to as "partridge." Mountie dove into the thick underbrush while I positioned myself along the possible flight path. Sure enough a "ruffie" exploded skyward and made a beeline for the nearest woods. But I was ready and the 20 gauge over-and-under "spoke" and the bird tumbled to the ground in a puff of feathers. Mountie did the rest and brought a lovely grey phase male ruffed grouse to hand.

I confess that I'm getting a bit lonely while I hunt late season ruffed grouse because it seems that I'm the only Manitoba hunter who takes advantage of this unique and wonderful hunting opportunity. A few years back the Manitoba Government extended the upland bird hunting season to the middle of December. That opened up a whole new world of ruffed grouse hunting since there's normally snow on the ground. You can track the birds, or at least know if there are any in the area.

Manitoba's ruffed grouse populations are in good shape, but the bird undergoes violent fluctuations in numbers; often mistakenly referred to as cycles. Cycles imply a certain regularity to the population changes, but I'm skeptical; Mother Nature just isn't that predictable! But it is safe to say that some years the woods are crawling with "ruffies" and in other years you are hard-pressed to find even one. Nobody has a good explanation for this phenomenon, and there's really nothing we can do about it. Luckily ruffed grouse are very prolific and normally have between nine and fourteen eggs, and if even half of them survive to adulthood, the falls woods can be almost be overrun with the birds. Which is a very happy development since many consider the ruffed grouse to be the finest eating wild game of all.

Mountie and Late Season Ruffed Grouse

And based on anecdotal reports, it appears that ruffed grouse numbers are on an upswing with hunters reporting good numbers, especially in the northern zones on the "agricultural fringe." Populations in the Duck and Porcupine Mountains seem especially good. One black bear guide told me that he regularly observed twenty birds per two kilometres when he was setting out baits in the Porcupines this spring.

The ruffed grouse is a bird of the young forest and thrives with commercial forestry. That was why I was not surprised at the reports from the Ducks and Porcupines. The aspen tree harvesting that has been going on there for a decade has created unbelievable ruffed grouse habitat, and I'm already looking forward to a trip there next fall. But apart from creating a varied forest there's really nothing we can do to manage this wonderful game bird; it manages quite well on its own.

Manitoba's upland bird hunting shuts down this weekend, but Mountie and I certainly intend to be out over the next few days; working the coverts and trying to flush the "king of the upland game birds." You might want to give it a try.

Caroline's favourite: Smothered Ruffed Grouse

Ruffed grouse is a family favourite. In fact, it was the first meat that our granddaughter Eden ate when she was a baby. Her mom and dad have a video of her taking her first taste of ground up grouse and the expression on her face was priceless as she tried to decide whether this new texture in her mouth was something she liked or not. Guess what... she loves it!!

This is son Tony's favourite recipe:

4 ruffed grouse - halved or cut breasts off of the bone flour salt and pepper to taste
1 tsp tarragon
1/4 lb butter
2 cups of sliced mushrooms (if you are lucky enough to have wild morel mushrooms, they add a wonderful flavour)
2 cups of sour cream at room temperature
1/2 cup chicken broth
1 Tbsp cranberry jelly

Put the flour, salt/pepper and tarragon in a bag. Toss the ruffed grouse halves, one at a time, in the bag until evenly covered with flour.

Melt 6 tablespoons of butter in skillet and brown the grouse.

Remove the grouse from pan and add remaining butter. Cook mushrooms in butter until browned. Return the grouse to the pan.

Mix sour cream, chicken broth and jelly. Pour over the grouse. Cover the pan and continue cooking until the grouse is cooked through.

Note: If you only use the breasts -- keep the carcass and boil in water for a wonderful broth to use in soups, sauces or gravy.

Serves 4

Try Hunting Teal This Year

(SEPTEMBER 2008)

One sure-fire way to maximize your outdoor pleasure is to hunt and fish in out-of-the-way places for species that are not sought after by everyone else. Take waterfowl hunting. Mallards and Canada geese are the marquee species that usually take top billing. And as much I like to pursue them, I realized many years ago that there was a lot more to waterfowling than just those two species.

Manitoba waterfowlers have at least thirteen other duck species to hunt ranging from the magnificent canvasback, to the dramatic bluebill, to those tiny marsh speedsters, the blue-wing and green-wing teal. Ever since the Province of Manitoba opened an early waterfowl season (that is restricted to Canadian resident hunters only), teal hunting opportunities have blossomed. Teal tend to head south earlier in the fall, especially the blue-wings, and were largely absent from Manitoba when the season opened in late September.

I've been seriously pursuing early-season teal for the last six years. And what a glorious time to hunt, and what glorious birds! The weather's warm, the leaves are golden, and the birds are abundant. Teal really like shallow water marshes and while wetland conditions looked grim early this year, summer rains caused Manitoba's wetlands to re-fill, creating oodles of teal feeding habitat. And to top it off, the rains really improved teal nesting success. Teal are real "upland" nesters and utilize hayfields to a great extent so the summer rains, which delayed haying, allowed a lot of teal ducklings to make it to the water. Overall, teal are abundant with blue-wings clocking in at a whopping 6.6 million breeding birds, forty-five percent over the long term average. Green wings, with almost 3 million breeding birds, are fifty-seven percent over the long term average.

The hunting suppliers have caught up with the teal craze and have stocked the shelves with tiny teal decoys that are a joy to carry. You can easily pack a dozen decoys in a smallish backpack and, since large decoy spreads are not required, it's real easy to set up your hunt.

Blue-wing teal are an ideal duck to start the youngsters on; the warm weather and the tendency of blue-wings to decoy make for an exciting first hunt. And since the birds are small, that new 20 gauge will be all the gun you need. And then there's the taste! Being early migrants, blue-wing teal really put on the fat during the month of August. By September, teal become little "butterballs" and are just about the tastiest duck on the planet. Caroline and I have nicknamed them "supper ducks" because they are a staple for our September supper menus.

Teal are quite easy to pluck, the Mandarin oranges of the duck world if you will. And I strongly recommend plucking teal as opposed to skinning since the plucking process preserves all of that savoury fat. And as for cooking teal, I recommend a really hot oven (500°F) and a short roasting time in a covered roaster; no more than twenty minutes. Or you can roast them in a closed barbecue at a very hot temperature on the top shelf. Make an aluminum foil "pan" to put them in so the fat does not drip into the fire. Otherwise you'll have flames.

So grab your lightest shotgun, and get out for an early season teal hunt. You won't regret it.

Caroline's favourite: Roasted Teal

> 4 teal
> Tangerines or Orange sections - enough to stuff teal
> 4 strips of bacon
> 3/4 cup of full bodied red wine such as a burgundy
> 1 Tbsp lemon juice
> 1 cup plum jelly (cranberry jelly works well too)
> 1/2 Tbsp flour
>
> Preheat oven to 400 degrees.

Salt and pepper birds inside and out. Insert tangerine or orange sections into cavity of bird. Wrap each bird with one slice of bacon. Place in roasting pan.

In a small skillet heat wine and lemon juice. Mix jelly into wine mixture until dissolved. Pour wine mixture over ducks.

Roast in 400 degree oven for 20-25 minutes. Baste birds every few minutes.

Remove ducks to platter.

Sauce (optional): skim off bacon fat. Add 1/2 tablespoon flour stirred into 2 tablespoons of water. Stir into the juices in the roaster. Simmer until sauce is thickened.

Note: I have made this recipe without using the bacon and actually prefer it as these little birds are quite tasty without the added bacon flavour. Either way works well.

MOUNTIE RETRIEVING A BLUE-WINGED TEAL

Big Game Hunting Much More Affordable than You Think

(August 2007)

Last week someone told me they hadn't taken up hunting because it was too expensive. I decided then and there to calculate once and for all just how *expensive* hunting was. But in order to make the numbers mean something, I had to find another activity with which to compare hunting. I chose golf which is exploding in popularity. And, I might add, providing tremendous feeding grounds for another explosion, that being Canada geese on golf courses.

I spoke to a salesman at a local sporting goods store and stipulated that I was looking at outfitting a new hunter at the moderate level; not too cheap but not necessarily super high-end. Heaven knows you can go crazy when it comes to high-end hunting gear!

"I know exactly what you are looking for," he said. "People are always pleasantly surprised at just how reasonable it is to become a hunter."

"For a big game rifle and scope there are some nice packages priced around the $450 dollar range," he explained. "These are good quality outfits that should last at least fifteen to twenty years."

He recommended a good pair of boots in the $200 range, which could also be used for general hiking. Rounding out the capital cost of the kit we added a blaze orange outfit and a backpack for about $150 for the both of them. We assumed that our aspiring hunter, being a Manitoban, would have the necessary cold weather gear. Add in a hundred dollars for miscellaneous gear (knife, calls, scents, etc.) and we arrive at a total capital cost for big game hunting equal to about $900. The other one-time expense is the cost of the federal and provincial firearms course which will run you about $100 so we can round it off at $1000 give or take. We assumed that our hunter would own a vehicle.

And as far as annual cost, a deer license is $34.67, and a box of shells will run about $25.

For information about golf I contacted a local golf pro.

"A decent set of clubs with a cart and a bag will run you about $350," he said. "Throw in two dozen balls at a buck apiece, shoes for $70 or so and some other miscellaneous stuff at $50 and you are set to go."

That adds up to $494 which we can round up to an even $500.00. And while this may make big game hunting look expensive, it's the annual costs for golfing that really add up.

The golf pro figured that the average golfer goes out about once every two weeks or about ten times over the season. And with green fees on average about $30, we're looking at an annual cost of $300 per year. That's a bare minimum since many people golf every week.

And we haven't even added on gas costs since many golfers travel far and wide to try various courses.

Now there are a lot of ways to slice this particular pie; there are golf club memberships and fancy clubs that could be added on or that extra vehicle cost for the four wheel drive truck you just have to have for hunting but those are all optional. So while it costs $500 to become a golfer versus about $1000 to be a deer hunter, the green fees can really add up negating the somewhat higher capital costs for big game hunting.

But, and here is the kicker, assuming you are a successful deer hunter, and with today's high deer numbers most hunters are, you will return home with a pile of juicy venison. And since you can't eat a golf scorecard, all of a sudden hunting doesn't look quite so expensive now, does it?

Trapping and the Fur Trade: Canada's Oldest Industry

(February 2004)

One of my great failings (and I have many) is that I am a hopeless romantic, especially about life in nature. My passion for the outdoor life was developed at the family cottage in the Whiteshell and honed by reading the boys' outdoor adventure books of the day. I eagerly devoured the African safari stories of the aptly-named J.A. Hunter and all others like it, but I was enthralled by stories of our great Northern wilderness.

Just thinking of Jack London's great stories like "To Build a Fire" or "The Law of Life" is enough to send shivers down my spine. Farley Mowat's *Lost in the Barrens* was read and re-read dozens of times, and *Cache Lake Country* by John J. Rowlands made me ache to live life in the bush. I wanted to be a trapper.

Fortunately good sense intervened, and I eventually got an education and became "normal" but my fascination with furbearers, trappers, and the trapping lifestyle has never waned. And my own experiences as a trapper—mostly a failed trapper if the truth be known—have given me profound respect for the men and women who actually make their living on the land.

Luckily I'm able to live out my trapping fantasies from time to time by matching wits with some of Manitoba's most clever creatures by trying to catch them. Trapping gives one a brand new perspective on nature because you literally have to think like a coyote or fox in order to outwit them. And the "stories in the snow" tell you exactly what happened. Nobody knows nature like a trapper.

A few years ago I had some power snares set for coyotes, and I was able to exactly see how those wily critters just walked around my sets time and time again. And these were on trails that they always used! Not only that I once saw where a lynx had walked along the same trail and obviously jumped right through the snare without making the "hair trigger" set spring. Talk about a ghost! I shook my head at that one.

Beaver trapping in winter is awesomely hard work. First you identify the feed pile and then you set your traps along the "runs" that the beavers have made going back and forth. It's no mean feat to try and figure out where those runs are under thirty centimetres or more of ice. Then if you get one, you've got to skin and prepare it. Beaver skins must be "fleshed," a job that takes an amateur like me about an hour. I'd rather skin a deer.

Then comes the selling of the fur, and the volatile fur market makes the stock market seem tame by comparison. That's because fur prices fluctuate wildly due to the whims of fur buyers and fashion designers.

This was brought home to me in spades a few years ago when I had the bright idea that I'd catch enough beavers to buy a black powder rifle. At the time they were about $30 each and I figured that about fifteen would do it. The romance of catching beavers to buy a musket was not lost on me! Well, to make a long story short I got about $8 each for my measly ten beavers when selling time came. So much for that idea!

Canada is synonymous with the fur trade, and our history is replete with the stories of trappers, trap lines, and the great fur trade routes. These are the "highways" that opened up a continent.

Canada is still the hub of the North American fur trade, and North American Fur Auctions are where most fur is sold. One could be forgiven for thinking that the fur business was on its last legs, but nothing could be further from the truth. Fur is "back", and sales are increasing especially to new markets in Asia and Russia.

One of the fascinations of the fur trade is the cultural connection created by this business. There is an unbroken line from the simple trapper's cabin in the remote Canadian wilderness to the fashion salons of Paris and London.

I continue to be a strong proponent of this most sustainable of industries. Of all of the things we humans do to make a living nothing touches the earth as lightly as the fur trade. I am heartened by the spirit of Canada's trappers who continue to stubbornly ply their trade in the face of a modern world that seems to have forgotten the real lessons of nature. *Meegwitch.*

Manitoba Beavers: The Good, the Bad, and the Ugly

(January 2006)

Canadians have a love-hate relationship with the beaver. Renowned as Canada's national animal, the demand to produce beaver hats for the fashion salons of Europe drove explorers across the continent in search of this furred treasure.

The beaver's Latin name, *Castor canadensis,* is derived from the "castor" glands located at the base of the tail. These scent glands are used by the animal to mark territory and are often removed from trapped animals to be dried and then sold into the perfume trade. And while not offensive, the odour of the castor glands is one you soon won't forget.

The beaver is superbly adapted to the wetlands and woodlands of North America and is best known for its ability to "engineer" its own environment. From dam building to the creation of immense "lodges," the beaver can take any flowing water and transform it into a pond deep enough and big enough to allow the animals to over-winter and thrive. And in this process they can denude an area of trees and cause flooding, something that does not endear it to farmers, landowners, and government officials alike. Beaver damage in Manitoba costs millions of dollars.

Many species of animals have adapted to these new beaver-created pond environments. A beaver pond's deep water can allow fish to over-winter in an area that would otherwise be devoid of fish; the partnership between brook trout and beavers is a classic example. And wood duck populations are expanding in tandem with the beavers' ponds. In dry years, beaver ponds can be the only water left in an area; a factor of critical importance to breeding water birds. But the flooding of wet meadows by beavers can destroy stands of sedge and grass species, food sources that can be very important for elk during the winter. There are always winners and losers in nature.

Beavers pair for life and are monogamous. Mating occurs in late winter, and the young are born after a three month gestation period. Litter sizes range from one to eight with two to four being the norm. The young stay with the parents for two years after which they are unceremoniously ejected from the pond to find, or create, their own habitats. This out-migration of two-year-olds explains the strange sight of lone beavers marching across a dry countryside as they search for a new residence. This is a time of high mortality since a small beaver out of water is easy pickings for a coyote. In fact, where beaver densities are high, as in Riding Mountain National Park, the animal makes up a high proportion of the summer diet of wolves.

Beavers are large, with adults weighing fifteen kilograms on average but Lancaster, Wisconsin, holds the beaver weight record with a forty-two kilogram monster that was trapped in 1960.

In fall, beavers ramp up their activity levels as they ready their lodges and food supplies for the winter. And it can be a shock to walk by what was a beautiful copse of poplars and see nothing but an overlapping mass of fallen trees. In fact I recall observing such a site with an anti-forestry activist who remarked that, "If a forestry company had done this we'd have them in court!"

The preparations for winter include building up the lodge; usually with mud from the bottom of the pond. I had the pleasure of watching that activity on one of my own ponds as I was waiting near the water's edge for an elk to pass by (it didn't). Just before dark, the beaver appeared and then dove to the bottom, re-surfacing with a pile of fresh mud clutched to its chest. Up the side of the house it waddled, awkwardly since its front paws were full of mud, and then plopped the mud on top of the house whereupon it proceeded to mortar it in place. I almost burst out laughing when on one of the trips the beaver fell flat on its face, a probable common occurrence. It just got up and stoically continued with its task. Getting ready for a Manitoba winter is no laughing matter.

The presence of a brushy "feed pile" poking up through the snow adjacent to a beaver house tells you that the house is occupied. The feed pile is stored food, often aspen branches that the beavers access throughout the winter. Beavers are quite active in the winter especially around the lodge. Their constant swimming means that despite freezing temperatures, the ice around the house can be very thin. Never walk up to a beaver house without constantly checking the ice thickness and be sure to avoid the feed pile altogether. I usually walk gingerly to the house from the shore side and jump on as soon as I can. Getting wet in winter can be very dangerous.

Our beaver populations are strong, and the animal is a permanent and usually welcome part of Manitoba's landscape.

Caroline's favourite (sort of)

In my early days of cooking game, I was a game girl to try cooking every possible game we had harvested using all the parts. My husband had drilled it into me that game must never be wasted! A favourite all round cookbook (and still is) is the *Northern Cookbook* that was first published in 1967 under the authority of the Minister of Indian Affairs and Northern Development, the Honourable Arthur Laing. There are many wonderful recipes in this book, and it is a great find for the beginner wild food cook.

Robert had decided to trap beavers this one winter. Out on our pond he set up his traps. He was fairly successful at this and was busy skinning the animals. Much to my dismay, I found the skins stretched and nailed to the floor of our loft in the house. The good thing was that we had not finished the flooring in the loft yet so no harm done. I looked at the remainder of the animal and started searching for recipes. Off to the trusty *Northern Cookbook* I went and low and behold if I didn't find a recipe for "fried beaver tail". I decided to try it. We had friends visiting us, and I decided to try it out on them along with roasted beaver meat. When tasting the meat, we were all sure we could taste the flavour of bark. And, when it came to eating the beaver tails, we all concluded that if you liked lard you might really like this recipe.

Fried Beaver Tail

- 2 beaver tails
- 1/2 cup vinegar
- 1 Tbsp salt
- 2 tsp Baking soda
- 1/4 cup flour
- 1/2 tsp salt
- 1/4 tsp pepper

1/4 cup butter
1/4 cup sherry or cooking wine
1 tsp dry mustard
1 tsp sugar
1/4 tsp garlic powder
1 Tbsp Worcestershire sauce

Skin beaver tails, clean thoroughly and wash well in solution of salt water. Let soak overnight in cold water to cover, adding 1/2 cup vinegar and 1 tablespoon salt to water.

Next day, remove from the brine, wash, then cover with a solution of 2 teaspoons soda to 2 quarts of water. Bring to a boil, reduce heat and simmer for 10 minutes. Drain.

Dredge beaver tails in seasoned flour.

Melt butter in heavy fry pan and sauté tails at low heat until tender.

Mix wine with mustard, sugar, garlic powder and Worcestershire sauce.

Add to beaver tails and simmer gently for 10 minutes basting frequently.

Mother and Daughter Preserve Family's Hunting Tradition

(DECEMBER 2003)

In a day and age when it seems that teenagers are only concerned about rockstars and video games, fifteen-year-old Marsha Dudar is definitely going against the grain.

Marsha and her family live on a small farm northwest of the picturesque village of Ethelbert, Manitoba. Their land is nestled against the Duck Mountains, a region abounding in wildlife. It's also settled by some of the most independent and hard-working people in Manitoba. I have a special affinity for those areas of Manitoba where farm meets forest. The people who live in such places possess an astonishing array of skills acquired while wresting a living from an often unforgiving countryside. And the Dudars are no exception.

When I spoke with Marsha and her mother, Darlene, I was struck by the array of activities that they are engaged in. Their 160 acre farm, augmented by leased crown land, supports a herd of 150 cows. Dad Dennis is a logging contractor in the Duck Mountains and supplies wood to various mills. Older brothers Dwight and Shawn complete this country family. The Dudars do all of those "country" activities that you'd expect from a farm family in such a varied landscape. They grow a big garden and preserve enough vegetables to comfortably see them through the winter. And of course they hunt.

"Hunting has always been an important family tradition," explained Darlene. "In fact, since we all hunt, we are able to provide enough wild meat for ourselves for the whole year." She chuckled when I asked about eating beef. "We eat beef now and then," she said. "But we find it much more economical to eat wild meat. Raising beef is our livelihood but eating wild meat is very special." And with Mother Nature's vast cornucopia of resources just outside their door, I could certainly see her point.

For Marsha, who grew up on wild game, it was only natural that, when she came of age, she would become a hunter. And, since her dad was often occupied with the family logging and farming businesses, it fell to Darlene to become Marsha's hunting partner. When I spoke with them, it was obvious that this was a partnership cherished by both, and days in the field only strengthened their relationship.

This fall Marsha downed a nice four-point buck that she and her mom called out from the woods. "It was a real foggy morning," Marsha recounted. "And as it got light we could see some does on the edge of the field. It was a perfect set up, so I worked the call and out came the buck, and I got him with one shot." Marsha uses a bolt action .222 because, according to her, "it doesn't kick much." So far in her hunting career Marsha has taken four deer, and it was obvious that Darlene was very proud.

The whole family, including Marsha, takes part in the preparation of the meat from cleaning and skinning the animal to cutting up the meat into the steaks and roasts. They also make homemade venison sausage and jerky; that spiced and dried meat that was a staple in pioneer times.

As they reminisced about their hunting experiences it became obvious that the taking of the animal was only one part of the whole hunting experience.

"The northern lights were very beautiful this fall," Marsha exclaimed. "They were flipping back and forth across the sky." Darlene pointed out that "We are always looking at the signs of nature, and we just soak it all in when we are out there."

Marsha is very involved with all the aspects of farm life from driving the tractor, to feeding cows. She has her own string of horses and a number are "show quality." So much so that Marsha was on the North West Regional 4-H horse show team. She shows cattle as well.

One can be forgiven for thinking that such lifestyles are mere anachronisms in this overwhelmingly urban society of ours. On the contrary. The Dudars' fierce attachment to their way of life, plus Dennis and Darlene's determination to pass it on to the next generation, tells me that the skills and attitudes developed on the farm are more valuable than ever. In spite of miracle technologies, MTV values, a video game culture, and the shallowness of most modern discourse, the ironclad rules of nature, family, and the cycle of life still apply.

This point is most certainly not lost on Darlene Dudar. "At this year's fair we entered a float in the parade that was all about how we lived," she explained. "And we had a great big banner on the side that said The Lifestyle Lives On."

And that's good to know.

Stacy Gets Her First Moose

(OCTOBER 2005)

The Peacock family of Powerview, Manitoba, eat, sleep, breathe, and drink the outdoors. From snowmobiling, to wilderness cottaging, to angling and hunting, this energetic family does it all. Parents Ken and Joanne and children Kayla (17), Stacy (16), and Drew (11) spend all their free time in the woods and on the waters in the Pine Falls area.

I met the family when Ken and I were employees in the Environment Department at the Pine Falls Paper Mill and spent many wonderful days in the field with them.

Ken and Joanne were determined that their children would become accomplished outdoors people. They caught fish at an early age and tagged along on all manner of outdoor adventures.

"Even when they were babies, we'd put them in bunting bags and bring them along on hunting and fishing trips," explained Ken. "They learned about the outdoors at an early age."

The Peacocks have a remote cottage on a lake north of Pine Falls which has become a family focal point. Remote cottages are just that; *remote*. And with no road, accessing the place requires work, but winter and summer, the Peacocks are there.

"Our whole family loves the taste of wild game," explained Ken. "And my kids are growing up on wild foods just like I did."

And given teenage appetites, it takes a lot of game to see these folks through the winter, which is why the annual moose hunt has become such a Peacock tradition.

For this year Ken took along his daughter Stacy as his moose hunting partner and, while this teenage marksman had already taken six deer in her hunting career, she had yet to bag a moose.

Stacy is a top student at Powerview School and is one of the only girls in the entire school who hunts.

"Being the only girl who hunts makes me a bit of an oddball," she explained. "And I even like to clean fish!"

On this particular moose hunt, Ken had been out with his other hunting partners and they did manage to bring home a moose and, after dropping the animal off at the locker plant, picked up Stacy after school and hurried back to the field. And after missing a moose the year before, she was bound and determined to be successful this year.

Stacy described the hunt as follows:

"We arrived at the hunting spot, launched our boat and drifted down the creek. And right after we left there were three moose on shore, and my gun wasn't even loaded! I was so nervous I could barely load, but finally I took aim and missed with my first shot. But the second and third shots were hits and down went my first moose! We were so excited! Dad said 'That was an A+, Stacy!' and gave me a big hug."

She continued: "We towed the moose in the water to a nice flat rock and used a "come-along" to winch him onto shore where we field dressed him."

I made the mistake of asking her whether that bothered her and she replied, "Of course not! And I made sure we saved the liver too since its real tasty! Then we cut the animal in half and had a tough job loading each half into the boats. But we did it."

She used her Dad's bolt action .270 rifle on the moose, but this determined girl is looking forward to buying her own gun.

"I have a part time job in town, and I've almost saved enough for my own rifle. I've decided to get a Savage bolt action 30-06," she explained.

Stacy described how important the outdoors were to her.

"I don't play any sports at school since I want to spend every weekend at the cottage or hunting and fishing with my family," she noted. "I especially love being outdoors with my dad."

Stacy has already decided on a career path.

"I want to be a conservation officer or biologist," she explained. "I'll definitely be a hunter all my life and a career in conservation would be pretty neat."

My own childhood is filled with wonderful memories of cottages, angling, and hunting and the joy of the outdoors has persisted to this day. It is a tribute to Ken and Joanne Peacock that their children are creating their own memories and traditions.

Caroline's favourite: BBQ Moose Kabobs

Moose roast - 3 lbs approximately
Greek marinade
Red Peppers
Green Peppers
Mushrooms
Red Onion
Zucchini

Cut up a moose roast into 1 1/2" cubes.

Marinate overnight (or to a maximum of 4 days) in a glass container in the fridge with your favourite greek salad dressing or use marinade recipe below.

Assemble your kabobs on skewers, alternating the meat with the vegetables. BBQ for approximately 8-10 minutes, brushing with marinade occasionally and turning frequently. Meat should be done medium. Do not overcook.

Marinade Recipe

1/4 cup olive oil
1/4 cup red wine vinegar (good quality)
2 Tbsp fresh lemon juice
1 Tbsp dried oregano
4 cloves of garlic, smashed and minced finely

Buying and Trying that First Shotgun

(JUNE 2005)

Youth waterfowl hunting programs have become a fall ritual, and true to form, it looks like even more young people will be introduced to the challenges of duck hunting. Interest in youth hunting programs is exploding in all regions of Canada.

Many of these young hunters will be clamouring for their own shotguns, which begs the question: "What is the best kind of shotgun to buy for a novice hunter?"

For some guidance, I contacted a salesperson at a local sporting goods store.

"Having a shotgun that fits is the most important consideration," he said. "I've seen too many kids show up at the youth hunts with Grandpa's trusty old 12 gauge only to have the gun kick like a mule. Getting the right shotgun is the start to an enjoyable hunt."

It may seem strange to talk about how a shotgun "fits", but fit is an important factor in most sporting gear. From hockey sticks to golf, clubs most seasoned players of all sports demand that their equipment be the right size and configuration for their bodies.

Shotguns are no different. Having struggled with ill-fitting shotguns early in my own bird hunting career, I can state categorically that a well-fitted shotgun is not only comfortable to shoot but is more accurate.

Shotgun fitting is filled with its own technical terms such as "drop" and "comb" and many more. Suffice it to say that shotgun fit is all about aligning your eyes parallel with the "sight plane" of the gun. In other words you should be looking straight along the top of the barrel and not at an angle up or down. For a more detailed description, just Google the words "shotgun fitting" and a number of excellent descriptive websites will pop up.

One of the biggest problems is that parents expect their young charges to use an adult-sized gun. More often than not the stock is way too long making the youngster stretch his or her arms too far.

In other words, most parents think like "hockey dads." So they shy away from buying a smaller-sized shotgun for Junior thinking that they will, like in the case of kids' goalie pads, have to soon buy another shotgun as the youngster grows. But unlike the case of goalie pads, all you need to do is replace the shorter gun stock with an adult version as the young person grows.

There are many choices for that first shotgun but a well-fitting shotgun that minimizes recoil should be the bottom line. A 12 gauge is probably the best first shotgun given its popularity, versatility, and shell availability.

You might be tempted to start a youngster off with a light shotgun assuming that this is what they could properly handle. But, paradoxically, nothing could be further from the truth. In fact, the lighter the shotgun, the heavier the kick. Heavier guns such as pumps, double barrels, and autoloaders are better "anchored" than the lighter single shots.

For reasons of reliability and looks, I prefer double barrels and tended to shy away from autoloaders since, to me at least, they seemed too complicated and hence unreliable. An autoloader uses the recoil of one shot to eject the spent shell and chamber the new shell. This results in much less kick as the recoil is dissipated in the action of ejecting the old round.

The salesperson at the sporting goods store laughed at me and noted, "You have those opinions about autoloaders, Bob, because you're an old guy. Today's autoloaders are very reliable and have come down in price considerably. Four to six hundred dollars can buy you a real nice auto."

The advantage of an autoloader is that the new shooter can concentrate on shooting and not worry about how to chamber the next round as in the case of a pump shotgun. The same is true of an over-and-under shotgun with a single trigger but these can get a bit pricey. Side-by-side doubles are traditional, but the wide sighting plane can be a distraction for the novice shooter.

So for all of these reasons, the rough consensus was that a parent could not go wrong buying that young shooter a 12 gauge autoloader with three-inch chambers. Today's shotguns usually come with interchangeable "chokes" that adjust the pattern of the fired shot which adds to the versatility. Of course you will need the proper federal and provincial permits and licences.

For reasons of safety, I would suggest that the novice start by just having one shell in the chamber for the first practise sessions. That way they would not have to worry about that second shot and concentrate on hitting that one target.

If you want to save money, try buying used. Most sporting goods stores have used shotgun sections and used guns can often be found in classified ads.

First Deer Stories

(April 2004)

Storytelling seems to be as much a part of hunting as the hunt itself. And since time immemorial hunters have recounted stories of "first deer."

One dad introduced his eleven-year-old son to deer hunting during the black powder season of 2003 as follows:

"My son and I were sitting in a ground blind along a field in southwest Manitoba. It was the Friday evening hunt, and we'd agreed to shoot bucks only as we still had another full day. I thought it might be cold (which it was), so I dressed James for winter. My oversight was not preparing for wet weather. We'd just sat down when freezing drizzle began and the wind was blowing it almost sideways. We had to make due with a plastic orange lawn bag with a hole to poke his head through.

"We sat like this, with no roof on the blind, for almost two hours. We talked a bit, and I kept being surprised that he wouldn't complain about being cold. Finally, just before sunset a couple of does wandered out within range, but we let them pass. Then the spike buck walked out and had no idea we were there. James gave me the nod; well actually it was a grin. I took aim and shot. The shot felt good, but with the smoke and the long grass I didn't see the deer go down. Fortunately we found it about where I'd shot it.

"It was my son's reaction that was most memorable. When we found the deer he had this expression of awe, surprise and excitement, which I might have expected. But, what really got me was his sense of accomplishment. We did what we had set out to do. It was just me and him, the weather was lousy, but we'd endured it. But by far the most important aspect was that this was the thing that, until now, the men in his life did—me, my dad and my friends. I think that James felt he'd become part of our fraternity that evening."

After the hunt, the father reflected on the bond that has developed between him and his son:

"I've been hunting for several years now and always hoped that one day my boys would show interest, but watching my son experience this was beyond anything I'd expected—it had such a huge effect on him and therefore on me. It may sound a little corny but this really was a rite of passage experience for him."

The next story was provided by my colleague Alan Tyrchniewicz, a thirty-eight-year old consulting economist who started hunting last fall. Here's what happened:

"A good friend of mine asked me to go to the archery range with him to practice shooting a bow. He suggested I give it a try. After a few shots, I was hooked. After several months of target practice, Chuck suggested that I go deer hunting with him. I was a little apprehensive because I wasn't sure if I was the hunting type. We scouted an area for about a month before the season, looking for signs of deer. We came across two nice bucks, one four-pointer and one five-pointer. I jokingly said that I'd take the bigger one.

"Friday evening, we went to our tree stands. Within an hour and a half, the two bucks had arrived. They wandered around just out of my comfort range for about twenty minutes. I was nervous because I did not want to wound the animal and have to track it for miles. I final mustered the courage and took the shot. It was true. The five-pointer was mine.

"I was lucky to have a good friend to take me out and teach me. We split the meat fifty–fifty, but I now have to figure out where to hang this velvet antlered head."

Tyrchniewicz's deer scored 125, large enough to place him in the archery hunters' hall of fame known as the Pope and Young record book. How's that for a first deer?

My nephew Mark Sopuck and his dad, Tim, enjoyed some quality time while deer hunting in the Whiteshell where the family cottage is located.

Mark's story:

"This deer hunt turned out to be much harder than I expected. The weather was absolutely frigid. By the end of the day, I was seriously discouraged. It might have been the cold weather, the lack of sleep or hearing too many deer hunting stories that had a different ending.

"The next morning on stand, the weather was much better. Suddenly, my dad whispered, "Mark! There's a deer!" Sure enough, a deer was standing in the middle of the creek. As I raised my gun the buck stopped. I had my sights on it and started the pull the trigger, but it didn't move. As I fumbled with the safety on Dad's rifle, he whispered, "Mark, shoot!" because the deer was one step away from going back in the bush. Its head was now behind a tree, but I still had a good view of its body. I took aim, and shot.

Mark's First Deer Taken in 2003

"We went to the spot where the deer was last standing, but there was no blood. After my Dad did some checking, he called me over and pointed down the trail. To my surprise, there was a form on the ground—my deer!"

Tim writes:

"Mark's first deer was definitely earned. Our hunt opened with the temperature at –20°C. Going on stand was simply brutal and the deer were not moving. Heavy overcast kept the temperature just below the freezing point that night. The next morning, as we crept into our blind overlooking a beaver flood, we felt like this could be *the day*.

"Sure enough, around nine, a buck appeared about seventy-five yards away. As it warily crossed a small opening, Mark took aim—but didn't fire! He was struggling with the safety and was getting flustered. Just before the deer was about to disappear into the woods, Mark recovered, took aim and squeezed.

"My heart leapt when I spotted the distinctive tawny shape, lying prone, just up ahead. As calmly as I could, I called Mark to my side. I'll never forget the size of his smile.

"As we hauled the deer back to the road, a group of hunters drove up and we exchanged pleasantries. When I mentioned that this was Mark's first deer, these strangers jumped out of the truck, and it was all handshakes, "Congratulations!" and "Tell us all about it, son." As it has been for countless generations passed, this was a profound event to be recognized, recounted and shared."

The Rewards of Being a Youth Hunt Mentor

(PREVIOUSLY UNPUBLISHED)

A wise man once said, "If you teach your kids to hunt, you won't have to hunt for your kids." Truer words were never spoken, and throughout human history—and pre-history for that matter—young men have been nurtured by senior hunters in the techniques, rites, and rituals of the hunt. And indeed the camaraderie, ethics, techniques, organization, and bonding of the hunt has been credited with developing human social structures. When you consider that, for 99.7 percent of humanity's existence on Earth, we were hunters, it is no wonder that we are hunters and gatherers at heart.

Many provinces have allowed special waterfowl and deer hunting seasons where hunting is restricted to young people between the ages of twelve and seventeen. My own direct experience as a youth hunt mentor is restricted to waterfowl so far, but I have talked to fathers who have been with their sons as they bagged their first deer.

In one case, I interviewed both the father and the son. The son excitedly recounted the experience from the pre-season scouting to the eventual taking and cleaning of the deer. I could sense what this meant to him, especially since he was with his dad. But it was the dad's comments that illustrated to me the enormity of the experience.

"This was one of the most profound experiences of my life," he recounted. "From the scouting to the kill, I could see his excitement and confidence build. And to be with him through this was a dream come true."

He went on to say, his voice choking with emotion, "No matter what happens in our lives, I will always have my son." That is how profound these experiences can be.

I have always envied teachers since they are often told by former students what a difference they made in their lives. How wonderful! Well, as a youth hunt mentor, I have been able to provide experiences to my "students" that they will never forget. And some have contacted me years later to tell me how profound that first hunt was for them.

Waterfowl hunting with young novices is magical; especially when accompanied by a good dog. At this point our young hunters have already taken a Hunter Safety course and their gun handling is impeccable. Many have been practising on clay pigeons and, with their quick young reflexes, are quite good shots. But nothing on the practise field can compare to the real thing. On the hunt day they are up as early as four AM—and these are teenagers! Usually we have scouted the marsh or field the day before, so the young hunters are keyed up to begin with. But nothing can compare to dawn in a duck blind. You stop the truck, and when you step outside you are greeted by the crisp fall air and, if you are lucky, the whistling wings of restless waterfowl trading between waterbodies. That really gets young hunters going. Boats are unloaded, filled with decoys and equipment, and quickly dragged to the marsh where a good blind must be found. A good blind must offer concealment plus an orientation to the wind so that the waterfowl will land into the decoys. The decoys are then placed accordingly and the long wait (it's only ten minutes but it seems an eternity!) begins for legal shooting time to arrive.

Finally, it's game on! The first birds pitch into the decoys and the mentor says, "Now!" The young hunters rise and usually empty their shotguns. And if their aim is true, a few birds are on the water. And on command the dog enters the water and brings back the birds. Few hunters use dogs in Manitoba, which is a pity since good dog work can make a hunt. And dogs add a dimension to a hunt that the young hunters soon appreciate, especially when your canine companion chases down a cripple or finds a bird concealed by tall and dense vegetation.

Usually we're done by ten and it's time to pack up. And after a hearty brunch, it's bird cleaning time! The kids usually are fascinated by these impromptu lessons in bird anatomy and eagerly take on what some consider a distasteful job. But one thing that is drilled into our young hunters is the need to respect the game, never waste wild game meat, and to prepare the birds in a manner that brings out the best in these delectable birds.

At around this time, the parents arrive to pick up our young hunters. I have been told afterwards that the drives home are one long hunting story as details of the hunt are excitedly relayed to the parents. So if you are an experienced hunter and have the chance to mentor a young person on their first hunt, do it. You will not regret it.

Ducks Pitching into Decoys

The Family that Hunts Together

(SEPTEMBER 2003)

Another waterfowl hunting season is upon us and the first people in the field were young hunters, ages twelve to seventeen, who have the first week of the season allotted just for them. They are able to take to the field in the company of experienced mentors who ensure a safe and ethical hunt. The mentors also provide valuable advice on shooting, decoy placement, and waterfowl identification.

One year I had a special request this year from our dear friend Terri Bessey whose husband, Mike, passed away in May. Mike, Terry and the kids, Lauren and Mason, were frequent family visitors to our place and most of the visits revolved around some kind of hunting or fishing.

"Would you take Lauren and Mason out hunting this year?" she asked. "I want to keep the hunting tradition alive in our family. Mike really wanted the kids to keep hunting." Terry is an avid hunter herself and often put Mike and me to shame with her shooting prowess. I immediately made the necessary arrangements for our hunting party.

Lauren is fifteen and retains that youthful exuberance that keeps you gasping for breath as you try and keep up. Mason, her younger brother, is still too young to hunt but insisted on coming along. Dressed in camouflage and blowing his duck call, Mason was determined to be part of the hunt. And he was, although I could sense in his eagerness a frustration at not being old enough to actually hunt. Soon, Mason, soon. Rounding out our little hunting party was nephew Mark Sopuck who, at fifteen, has become quite an experienced hunter. But the ducks were tough and hard to hit, even for good shots like these two teenagers.

We sat in the blind in the morning and picked up two birds which were nicely retrieved by Rex, their English Springer Spaniel. After the marsh hunt we "jumped" some potholes. The kids really liked this style. First you spot the ducks and slowly try and sneak up and flush them or you encircle them and one person tries to flush them over the guns. There was much laughter because, no matter what our elaborate plans were, the ducks mostly didn't fly where they were supposed to. But at one pothole it all worked and the two young hunters got three beautiful blue-winged teal. Mason gave the right commands to Rex, and the dog made a fine triple retrieve. Terry and I were grinning from ear to ear as we saw the wonder in the kids' eyes as they admired the birds' plumage and the laughter as they re-lived the flush and the shots.

Back at the farm as the kids were packing up to go we got a surprise phone call from Minnedosa. Lauren had been picked for the Stonewall 12/20 goose shoot to be part of the all-girl "dream team" for 2004. "Wow," she said. "I've always wanted to go goose hunting."

As we sat in the living room reflecting on the morning's events, I remarked on how much Mike would have loved to have been here with his family. Terry looked at me with a small smile and said, "Mike is here."

The North American Model of Wildlife Management

(FEBRUARY 2009)

Maybe it's just age, but our long, but wonderful, Manitoba winters often cause me to reflect on years past. Last fall one of my great pleasures was to re-connect with my son-in-law, Graham Street, who is quickly becoming a most skillful hunter.

Graham and I shared many a joyous day in the duck marsh, the grouse cover, and the deer woods. These experiences were made even more memorable because Graham is a transplanted Englishman whose family emigrated in the 1990s. And what we shared in Manitoba's outdoors would not be possible in the United Kingdom and across much of Europe. There, wildlife is essentially owned by the landowner and hunting is largely reserved for the wealthy.

Manitobans tend to take our fish and wildlife resources for granted. We "common people" have access to vast tracts of Crown land and thousands of lakes and rivers. We tend to think nothing of grabbing our fishing, hunting and outdoor gear and heading out for a day in the field. I know, some of us gripe about how "expensive" this has become, but before we complain too much, just think of what these activities cost in the "old country," if they are indeed even possible.

Public ownership of fish and wildlife, referred to as "common property resources," came about because the European settlers made a conscious decision NOT to replicate the European model of wildlife management but strived to ensure that all citizens had access to fish and wildlife. It started well, but as the human population expanded and hunting technology improved, populations of some game species became severely depleted. This has been coined the *"tragedy of the commons,"* a process whereby common property resources are depleted because no one has an interest in conserving them, only in harvesting them. A recipe for disaster if there ever was one.

Pre-eminent Canadian wildlife scholar, Dr. Valerius Geist wrote:

"The North American Model of Wildlife Conservation arose at the beginning of the 20th century in response to the virtual decimation of wildlife across most of the North American continent by the end of the 19th century."

It is hard to appreciate, these days, just how dire the wildlife situation was a hundred years ago. Our main wildlife *problems* these days usually relate to over-abundance such as the management of Canada geese, too many bears in campgrounds, increases in wildlife-vehicle collisions, predation on livestock, and the control of diseases resident in some abundant wildlife species.

Young waterfowl hunters, for example, find it hard to believe, but bagging a Canada goose in the 1960s was a very big deal—and now they are virtual plague in some areas.

Geist attributes the success of the North American model to grassroots democracy whereby everyone, especially hunters and anglers, have an interest in conservation. Couple this with better science and more effective regulations and the results are obvious.

And as Geist notes:

"The return of wildlife and biodiversity to the continent of North America is probably the greatest environmental achievement of the 20th century and the North American Model of Wildlife Conservation one of the greatest achievements of North American culture."

And thanks to the North American Model— and the work of those great conservationists of the past—the "good old days" for many species of wildlife are right now.

The Paradox of Hunting

(March 2009)

Like many of you, I am sent a lot of newspaper articles and columns via the Internet, and a recent one from the Washington Post piqued my interest. Entitled "Major Decline Found in Some Bird Groups," the article described dramatic declines in the numbers of many bird species such as songbirds and shorebirds according to "The State of the Birds" report issued by the US Department of the Interior. But the byline under the article noted "But Conservation Has Helped Others." This all begs the question about why some species are declining while others are increasing.

After the bad news examples, the article went on to describe bird conservation success stories and, lo and behold, noted that: "hunted species and iconic species such as the bald eagle have expanded in numbers…" The report also notes that: "taken as a whole the 39 species of hunted waterfowl that federal managers track have increased 100% over the past 40 years."

One might be tempted to ask how this can happen; that hunted bird species are by and large doing better than those that are not hunted? After all, millions of ducks and geese are annually harvested across North America and one thing we can be sure of; a bird that's in my freezer won't be flying south!

The "paradox of hunting," whereby hunted species generally fare better than other species, be explained very simply. Waterfowl, and indeed all of our game species, have a motivated and committed constituency that works tirelessly on their behalf. Hunters have time and time again "stepped up to the plate" when it comes to helping the species they cherish. Hunters spend money, some three billion dollars in the last twenty years for waterfowl conservation alone, and have devoted countless hours to wildlife conservation. From erecting nest tunnels for mallards, to improving big game habitats, and to urging governments to devote more resources to wildlife conservation and wildlife science, hunters are tireless in their conservation advocacy. We even begged to be taxed for wildlife conservation!

Now to some this may just be self-interest at play, but my response to that challenge is "well, what of it?" Hunters are unique in the conservation world in that we treasure abundance. One flock of mallards is not enough for us; we wish to see the skies filled with birds. We want to see a steady parade of deer go past our stand as we wait for that perfect shot. And while it may be in my self-interest as a deer hunter to protect and manage deer habitat, that deer habitat also provides society with multiple benefits in terms of songbird conservation and better water management to name just two.

Indeed if we look at the entire suite of hunted species across North America, we see species that are increasing in number or holding their own at fairly high levels. Antelope have returned to the great grasslands of the west, wild turkeys keep expanding their range, elk have increased dramatically, while flocks of geese can darken the sky.

The North American model of wildlife conservation works. Public ownership of wildlife coupled with a motivated and committed hunting constituency creates the conditions for government action and private conservation. Add in sound science, and the results are there for all to see.

The Man who Changed the Face of Conservation

(August 2008)

I was first introduced to the writings of Aldo Leopold (1887–1948) in the mid 1970s. At that time I was a graduate student in the Natural Resources program at Cornell University. A professor gave us a reading assignment featuring the writings of this great conservationist. Leopold is considered to be the father of wildlife management in North America and was a lifelong fisherman and hunter.

Leopold's seminal work, *A Sand County Almanac,* takes its name from the little 120 acre "sand farm", as he affectionately called it, that the Leopold family owned in Wisconsin. My own dog-eared copy of this treasured book has a special place on my bookshelf, and I'm still gleaning knowledge every time I open its tattered pages. And it's always gruesomely funny to see my 1974 margin notes. "Was I really that pompous back then?" I ask myself.

Leopold was the Professor of Game Management at the University of Wisconsin, and it was here that he honed his view of man's place in the natural world. He loved wild nature and wild places and his first words in the foreword read, "There are some who can live without wild things and some who cannot. These essays are the delights and dilemmas of one who cannot."

The first part of *A Sand County Almanac* (and I highly recommend the book) describes a year in the life of the little "sand farm." Leopold takes the reader from the depths of winter to the bursting glory of spring, to the magnificence of summer, and back to the melancholy of fall and winter. His scientist's eye for detail coupled with a poet's heart and a superb writing style make you feel like you are there with him. These are his delights of the natural world.

Much of the rest of the book is taken up with trying to figure out humanity's place on this earth and how we can reconcile our demands on Nature with our needs to conserve those ecological processes that we must have in order to survive. These are Leopold's "dilemmas."

Leopold's conservation work reached all the way into our home province, and in his "Manitoba" chapter he describes his time on Clandeboye Bay at our famed Delta Marsh on the south shores of Lake Manitoba. Leopold was brought to Delta Marsh during the "Dirty Thirties" by Minnesota businessman, and President of General Mills (the "Cheerios" company), James Ford Bell to advise Bell on how to conserve the dwindling flocks of waterfowl. Bell owned much of Delta Marsh and treasured the waterfowl hunting that the marsh provided. Bell's guiding philosophy was "to put two birds back for every one I take."

Leopold convinced Bell that in order to conserve waterfowl you had to know as much about them as you possibly could. And so was born the famous waterfowl research facility at Delta Marsh. Funded by Bell, Delta Marsh soon became a Mecca for waterfowl researches from around the world. And the first Director on the Research Station was a graduate student of Leopold's, H. Albert Hochbaum.

Unfortunately, Delta Marsh has been severely degraded by the Portage Diversion and the regulation of Lake Manitoba; one of those conservation "dilemmas" that would so have vexed Leopold. Nevertheless, Leopold left the world a much better place that he found it. We should all be so fortunate.

Surviving a Tough Winter

(FEBRUARY 2009)

One of the great things about being a hunter is the kinship that one feels with your prey. Take the white-tailed deer. Even though white-tails can adapt to many different environments, a Manitoba winter has got to rank up there as one of the white-tail's greatest challenges.

This was evident on a recent ski through my "bush quarter" where about a dozen white-tails are spending the winter. The "story in the snow" told where they fed, what they ate, and where they bedded. Not to mention the telltale bounds through the snow that told me that I had been detected long before they even saw me.

The over-wintering success of Manitoba's white-tails is of more than academic interest since winter survival has got a lot to do with the numbers of deer we will see in the fall.

So, how do white-tails make it through a Manitoba winter? The fact that so many do is made even more remarkable when you consider that white-tailed deer are only recent immigrants to this province. The white-tail marched west with the European settlers, adapting well to the new agricultural landscape and displacing the native mule deer. One could say that they don't even belong here!

In order to learn more about how these deer survive a Manitoba winter, I contacted Brian Ransom, biologist and Manitoba's former Minister of Natural Resources, and Herb Goulden Manitoba's former Deer Manager. Both of these gentlemen eat sleep, breathe and drink white-tail deer and are an endless source of deer information.

Goulden noted that fat to a deer is like fuel to a car. The more fat (fuel), the longer the deer (car) can go. Deer "fill up" in the fall and lay down significant reserves of fat for the winter. I can confirm Ransom's observation that all deer are 'rolling with fat" in the fall. Manitoba's agricultural landscape sets a bountiful fall table for white-tails. There are grain crops of course along with the highly nutritious oilseeds and legumes like sunflowers and field peas respectively. Throw in alfalfa and acorns if available and that is a food mix guaranteed to fatten up any deer.

According to Ransom, deer will switch to snowberry or "buck brush" at the onset of winter and eat the nutritious white berries. As winter wears on those deer with access to crops, spilled grain, or hay continue with that diet. Ransom notes that he always gets a group of deer in his corrals sharing feed pellets with the horses.

For deer with little or no access to agricultural crops, like those in my "bush quarter" it's a different story. They have to calculate whether eating is even worthwhile. Goulden says that white-tails have a unique ability to slow their metabolism and enter into phase that has been dubbed "walking hibernation." A slow metabolic rate conserves energy, allowing the fat reserves to last longer. While in this state deer forgo certain foods or eating altogether because the energy gained may be less than the energy expended to eat it. In extreme conditions deer spend a lot of time curled up and bedded down, counting on their thick, hollow-haired coats to keep them warm.

Goulden notes that the "moments of truth" for deer are when the snow comes and when the snow goes. As well, even though we may like a February thaw, that's bad for deer because the warm weather can "trick" a deer's metabolism into speeding up too soon and using more energy. A late March storm can catch the deer in a weakened state and hasten their demise. The prolonged cold spell this winter actually helped by keeping their metabolism slow and conserving energy. If the weathers warms and stays that way, the deer are home free. But a late winter storm or rain can kill the most vulnerable.

Northern white-tails are also much larger than their southern cousins. On a recent trip to Texas, I marvelled at their skinny deer as compared to our Manitoba "monsters." Large body mass conserves energy.

The most vulnerable deer are the fawns which simply do not have enough body mass and the big bucks who have lower reserves of fat due to their exertions in the fall rutting season. Goulden recalls the times that he came across dead fawns and bucks. "They just died in their beds of hypothermia," he said.

Goulden feels that the deer of today survive tougher winters than the deer of thirty years ago because of the rich mix of agricultural foods that are now available to them.

All hunters are awe-struck by this marvellous animal. As Ransom notes, "White-tailed deer are more responsible for my connection to the land than any other animal. They continue to fascinate me."

And me as well.

Waterfowl Hunters' Gift to Mother Nature

(April 2005)

For most North American waterfowlers, mallard hunting is duck hunting, pure and simple. And the sight of big drake mallards, or greenheads, sifting into a decoy set stirs the hearts of duck hunters like no other bird. The mallard is North America's most common duck, but the species is in need of a helping hand, especially in Prairie Canada where habitat loss and an "out-of-balance" predator community has reduced the ability of mallard hens to bring off a successful nest. Only one out of ten nests actually results in a clutch of ducklings.

Mallards are aggressive "re-nesters," and make many attempts to bring off a clutch. Mallards are also a bird that nest almost anywhere from over the water, to grasslands and sometimes in tree cavities. It is this last trait that duck managers have begun to exploit in an attempt to improve mallard nest success.

Nest tunnels, often called "hen houses," are tunnel-shaped artificial nest structures placed over the water in a manner to make them "predator proof." These "duck tunnels" are attached to metal posts which are pounded into the shallow water near the edges of wetlands.

Matt Chouinard, a Staff Biologist with the Delta Waterfowl Foundation (DWF) based in Minnesota, conducted Masters level research on the optimum use of henhouses.

DUCK NESTING TUNNEL

"In my study area near Minnedosa, Manitoba, nest success went from a low of 50% to one year where 99% of my tunnels kicked out a mallard brood," explained Chouinard. "That's a far cry from the 2% to 5% nest success experienced by ground nesting ducks in that area."

He went on to note that, "Installing two hen houses per small wetland seemed to work best and we had the best luck when the tunnels were on the north or west side of the wetland somewhat protected from the wind."

Of course the real test of a wildlife management technique is what effect it has on the overall population and there are indications that the hen house program near Minnedosa is paying big duck dividends. Dan Coulton is another Delta student who is completing a PhD that looked at the effects of hen houses on mallard populations. Coulton's study showed some very positive results.

"My top-performing model said that tunnel recruits were important to the Minnedosa mallard population," Coulton says. "Of the banded juvenile females I recaptured during the study, eighty-nine percent hatched in Hen Houses the previous year."

The hen house program is expanding all across North America and to date there are over 4,000 structures in Manitoba, Alberta, Ontario, North Dakota, Pennsylvania, Michigan, Colorado, and Utah with new projects in Minnesota, Iowa, and Saskatchewan coming on stream. And with an average of four ducks produced per hen house according to Chouinard's study, that a whopping 16,000 new mallards every year. Not bad!

Hen houses are ideal conservation projects for wildlife associations and youth groups to take on. Now is the time to build them and then installation would occur in March or April while the ice is still on the wetlands allowing for easy travel.

Hardy Transplant Thriving in Manitoba

(July 2010)

"Steady, boy, steady," I whispered to my bird dog Mountie who was behaving very "birdy" on this warm September afternoon in southeastern Saskatchewan. With his head low to the ground, Mountie pieced out the scent trail. The reward was an explosive flush of over twenty Hungarian partridge from a copse of trees not fifteen metres from me. I still get unnerved by this, even after decades of bird hunting, but I did have the presence of mind to hold off shooting since the covey wheeled towards my hunting partners. But yet again I was forced to marvel at the hardy Hungarian partridge, or "Hun" as he is often called, which has become such a delightful addition to Manitoba's bird community.

Huns are native to Western Eurasia, from Britain east to northern Russia and south to southern Europe, Turkey, northern Iran, and Mongolia. In the early 1900s this hardy survivor was released into North America and has been with us ever since. Huns adapted best to the High Plains, an area similar to that from where they originated. The bird is actually increasing both in terms of range and numbers, much to delight of upland gunners everywhere. And just last week Caroline and I were thrilled to see a Hungarian partridge brood, and two anxious parents, just south of Riding Mountain National Park, an area where they had not been known to frequent to any great extent. The sparrow-sized little ones ran down the road in front of us only to flush strongly back into the crop of wheat. "There go some survivors," I commented to Caroline.

FLUSHED HUNS AND GUNNER

This "two parenting thing" is unique among upland birds. The males of most upland bird species such as ruffed and sharp-tailed grouse, for example, go to great lengths to attract a female. But after mating, the female is left to hatch the clutch and look after the young on her own. Not so with Huns where the males sticks around and helps carry the load to bring off a successful batch of offspring. These "family groups" stick together for much of the rest of the year but only about half of the young survive until fall. It's a good thing that Huns can lay up to twenty eggs! For the first ten days or so the young subsist solely on insects, growing rapidly on this high-protein diet. They then become seed eaters for the rest of their lives, and do very well on agricultural crops like wheat. In fact, their ability to adapt to grain agriculture, where cover is often scarce, is one of their saving graces. I think that new modern farming methods, such as zero-tillage and winter wheat, have been significant contributors to the expansion of the Hungarian partridge. Both agricultural practices increase the amount of nesting cover, which until now, was probably a limiting factor for the little Hungarian partridge. The bird's habit of moving into farm yards in the winter helps too. Not only are predators scarce in farm yards, but the spilled grain makes for very nutritious winter food. In fact abandoned farmyards are considered ideal for Huns and veteran upland bird hunters deliberately key in on these "habitat oases."

We ended up doing very well on our Hungarian partridge hunt in southeastern Saskatchewan, an area that is tailor-made for this little speedster. I highly recommend that you add a Hungarian partridge hunt to your schedule this fall.

Eat Beef If You Care About Environmental Conservation

(February 2010)

Lloyd Thompson turned to me from the driver's side of the pickup truck, flashed a genial grin and said, "Well, Bob, how do you like my little ranch?"

Lloyd, his wife, Jean, and three generations of Thompsons ranch near Carnduff, in southeastern Saskatchewan, and epitomize the generosity, kindliness and rugged independence of ranchers everywhere. His "little ranch" description belies the 15,000 acres and 1,000 cows that comprise the Thompsons' T 4 Ranches Ltd.

A friend and I were hunting the native sharp-tailed grouse on T 4 Ranches, and we were taken on a pickup truck tour of the "little ranch" by Lloyd Thompson prior to the hunt. And it was astonishing. Wave after wave of sharp-tails were flushing from the tall grass fields we were slowly traversing. To many ecologists, the sharp-tailed grouse is an indicator of an ecosystem's health. You might ask what the connection is between T 4 Ranches and sharp-tailed grouse. The answer to that question, funnily enough, starts on the dinner plates of the nation.

In spite of urbanization, our society is completely dependent on the products of the countryside. Or as one wag put it, "If you eat, you are part of agriculture." What you eat determines what farmers and ranchers produce. In addition, what they produce has profound implications for landscape conservation since each food production system has differing effects on soil, water and wildlife. Some systems are much better than others in terms of landscape conservation, with beef cattle ranching, T 4 Ranch style, being the very best of all.

Cows efficiently convert grass and hay, non-human food, to people food. Big deal you say. However, grass and hay are perennial plants that cover the land with a permanent layer of vegetation that prevents soil erosion during rains and windstorms, and they provide habitat for wildlife such as nesting ducks, songbirds and my beloved sharp-tailed grouse. Extensive beef production in ranch country is an agricultural system that promotes animal welfare, landscape conservation and wildlife preservation.

Critics of the cattle industry cite the plight of the rainforest, methane production and overgrazing as reasons to shut down the cattle industry, all the while ignoring the landscape conservation benefits of well-managed, extensive cattle ranching. To be blunt, cattle create an economic incentive to conserve, manage and create diverse and productive grasslands. Those great, and seemingly boring, vistas of native prairie in Saskatchewan and Alberta (often contemptuously dismissed as "drive-through country") represent a treasure trove of wildlife and biodiversity, one of the great natural wonders of North America. And it is still in existence because of ranchers.

Meanwhile, back at T 4 Ranches, this landscape conservation process was magically rolling out before our very eyes. That is because Thompson's "hobby" is to purchase cultivated grain land and "sow it down" to hay and pasture for cattle feed. All that perennial cover creates lots of room for nesting birds and other wildlife that easily co-exist with the extensive ranching and grazing that predominates on T 4 Ranches.

This leads us to another favourite argument of the cattle critics, namely that humans should bypass meat and consume the plant products of the land, thus ensuring more efficient use of the Earth's resources. The problem with that argument is that not all hectares are created equal. We have millions of hectares of sandy, sloping and fragile land that will produce grain crops for a few years, but as the soil is played out, higher and higher levels of inputs are required to grow crops during this downward spiral of soil degradation. Much better to have such fragile land covered with a conservation blanket of perennial vegetation that is cropped by a well-managed cattle herd. By the way, for the holier-than-thou tofu eaters out there, your dietary preference encourages the expansion of row-crop soybean production, often at the expense of native grasslands. No tofu will ever find its way into our home; we care too much about the land.

As for the red meat is bad for you argument, I take the view that if you give up fat (and sugar and alcohol, too, for that matter) you may not live longer; it will just seem that way. Make your own call on that one, but I am here to live a little. As Clifton Fadiman wrote, "I have yet to meet a man who, with a good *tournedos Rossini* inside him, was not the finer for it, the more open to virtuous influences."

So, when you are about to tuck into a big juicy steak, ponder what it represents. That meal of Canadian ranched beef has contributed to landscape and wildlife conservation and kept generations of land stewards like the Thompsons in the ranching business for the benefit of all of us.

As for our final tally of sharp-tailed grouse, let us just say beef was on the menu that day.

Food for Thought

(May 2008)

Over the last few years there have been a number of articles examining the future of hunting and wild game as food. As I read some of these articles, which look at the factors affecting today's hunters, I started thinking about where some of tomorrow's hunters might arise. But before I get to the "meat" of this essay, I'd like to pass on some recent observations:

- Recently, the lifestyle section one of Canada's national newspapers included a chef's column on cooking venison. Before he got to the recipe, the chef fondly recalled family hunting trips he experienced as a boy in Italy.

- The Food Channel's *Iron Chef America* is a duel between two world class chefs who must present blue-ribbon dishes to a panel of judges in under an hour, using the show's "secret" ingredient. Recently, venison was featured and, as an ingredient, it received rave reviews by the chefs, commentators and judges.

- Jamie Oliver, one of the Food Network's young superstars, just came out with a cookbook, *Jamie Cooks at Home*. It contains a section on wild game, including an essay explaining his support for hunting.

- James Pollan's recent book, *Omnivore's Dilemma*, is one man's exploration of food production and consumption. Part of his journey is a wild boar hunt, a fulfillment of his need to walk the path of seeking, harvesting, processing and eating his own meat. To the author's amazement, hunting revealed itself to be a profound and intensely satisfying experience.

CAROLINE AND MOLLY ON A COLD MORNING DUCK HUNT

And now we can add in those wildly popular television shows, warts and all, such as *Duck Dynasty, Mountain Men, Alaska; The Last Frontier*, CBC's *Land and Sea*, and many other knock-offs on YouTube.

What do these snippets from popular culture mean to hunters? Studies show that hunters' main motivators include being in the outdoors and close to nature, sharing memorable experiences with friends and family and procuring wild meat. These motivations are so ingrained that we rarely bring them up in conversation with non-hunters.

But we should. There is a growing segment in society that values the nutritional qualities, the unique flavours and the connections to the natural world that come with wild game. My niece studied human nutritional sciences and tells me that wild venison is high in omega three fatty acids and low in saturated fat and cholesterol.

As well as being a healthy choice, wild meat, to use the vernacular of our times, is organic, free-range and locally-harvested. It's a challenge to find meat like that your local supermarket. I have no problem with the quality of meats produced by conventional agriculture, but hunters have the good fortune of bringing home a premium product whose qualities are increasingly appreciated by non-hunters.

There is a developing backlash in urbanized society to its remoteness from food production and the natural world. Some city dwellers, wishing to connect directly with their food, are becoming intrigued by hunting as a recreational pursuit. When you think about it, hunting "re-creates" some of the hunter-gatherer experience that defined 99% of human existence. Hunting is one of the truly "authentic" experiences we have left in this modern, sanitized world.

I'm not expecting a stampede to the hunting license counter, but I am encouraged by the growing interest in knowing where our food comes from. When our non-hunting friends visit, Caroline and I are happy to introduce them to our organic, free-range, locally-harvested wild bounty, and I encourage my fellow hunters to do the same.

Do-It-Yourself Venison Steaks and Roasts

(December 2007)

Manitoba's licensed hunters take between 25,000 and 30,000 deer each fall, which represents a lot of very high quality meat. And unlike other outdoor pursuits, deer hunting actually makes economic sense. A mature white-tail buck will produce about 50 kilograms of superb meat which is worth about $300 at an average price of $6 per kilogram.

Of course, deer hunting is about much more than economics, and at our house, making venison roasts and steaks has become a cherished fall tradition. However, many Manitoba hunters forgo preparing their own venison thinking that butchering a deer is difficult. It's actually quite easy.

Skinning your deer is the first step. It should be hanging by its hind legs with the head off the ground. Deer are easiest to skin when they are still warm but I prefer to leave the skin on until I decide to cut it up. This makes the skinning process more difficult but precludes the development of a dried outer layer of meat.

The next step is to split the deer down the backbone into halves. Formerly, I used a carpenter saw, which works surprisingly well, but have now settled on an electric reciprocating saw. I highly recommend reciprocating saws for splitting deer. The thin blade makes a neat cut and they are powerful enough to cut bone easily.

Once the carcass is split, count five or six ribs up from the hind quarter and cut across the half to make your quarters. I cut the ribs off about 12 cm from the backbone and that meat goes for stew, burger or sausage. Now take the hind quarter and start cutting steaks off the backbone. Doing your own steaks means that you can select the exact thickness you want. I recall my surprise at my very first steak many years ago: "Gee it looks just like a miniature T-bone!" Which, of course, it was.

Some deer hunters completely "de-bone" the animal including the steaks. We used to do that but have now opted to keep the bone in our steaks. We just like them that way, and the reciprocating saw cuts steaks very well. As far as the roasts go, we take them only off the hind quarters. Lately, instead of cutting across the grain, we have taken to separating the muscles there which creates roasts like you see in the supermarkets.

We wrap each piece twice, once with plastic and once with freezer wrap. Finally, and I cannot stress this enough, we label and date each piece before freezing. All of the rest of the meat, front quarters included, is trimmed. Some we make into deer burger at home where we mix it with pork fat. The rest is taken to the butcher's to be made into sausage, garlic rings, pepperoni or whatever else strikes our fancy.

Caroline Cutting Deer

For more details on butchering your own deer, go to www.chefdepot.net which has a good diagram of the cuts on a deer. There are also instructional videos on YouTube; just do a search of that site under the phrase, "how to butcher a deer."

As Dr. Lee Foote from the University of Alberta says: "We hunters find it gratifying, in a spiritual realm, to take responsibility for our food." Preparing your own deer meat extends the hunting process and expands the enjoyment from the field right to the kitchen. And you'll learn a new skill too!

Caroline's favourite: Venison Roast

Often we hear people say that they find venison tough and don't care for the texture. Venison is a wonderful game meat but must be cooked like lamb. The fat is similar to lamb and for a roast and steak, it must be served on a warm platter or plate. Venison roasts and steaks should be cooked to medium rare at the most.

One favourite way to do a roast is on the rotisserie. You don't even need to marinate. We like to use a rub.

Rub

2 tsp black peppercorn ground
1 Tbsp crushed rosemary
1 Tbsp parsley flakes
2 garlic cloves minced
1 Tbsp olive oil
Spread rub over the roast.
Insert roast onto skewer for rotisserie.

Cook 20–25 minutes per pound (meat thermometer should read 140°F degrees for medium rare). Remove from skewer and allow to rest on warm platter for 10–20 minutes. Slice thinly.

Preparing Wild Game for the Table

(October 2004)

When I ask people if they have ever eaten wild game, they either respond that they would like to try it, "But I've heard it's gamey." Or they say, "I tried deer (or goose, duck etc) once, and it was real gamey." The word "gamey" has a negative connotation and implies that the wild meat was either too strong or too dry or both for that matter.

No wild meat is "gamey" by nature. That only happens when the animal is not properly cared for after the kill.

Looking after wild game not only makes for a much better meal, but is part and parcel of being an ethical hunter. "Eating what you kill" is not just a flippant term applied to the behaviour of aggressive stock brokers but denotes respect for animal. Quite simply, it is every hunter's solemn and sacred duty to never waste game due to improper handling.

Fortunately, Manitoba's cool autumns are forgiving in terms of game handling; the low temperatures give our hunters a latitude that their counterparts, in the warmer climes of the Southern States for example, do not have.

One iron-clad rule for all game animals is that the meat needs to be cooled quickly. The opening weekend for sharp-tailed grouse is usually in mid-September when temperatures can often reach 25°C. And not only are these temperatures hard on hunters and dogs, they can also affect the meat. I extract the entrails of the birds as soon after they are shot as I can. I also stuff a bit of grass into the body cavity to ensure that air can get inside. Not only do we cool the birds off quickly, but we have the whole birds for pictures at the end of the day.

For ducks and geese, one should also take the entrails out as soon as possible or even go so far as to pluck the birds in the field. Not only does this reduce the work time at home, but also cools the birds.

Once the cleaned birds are home, I soak them overnight in heavily salted water. The brine draws any blood out of the meat caused by the shot. I suspect that blood in the meat is the real cause of any "gamey" taste in birds. Just make sure that, prior to freezing, you rinse the birds well, or you will get a real salty surprise at dinner time.

It is even more important for big game that the animal be cleaned as soon as possible. It is amazing how warm the body cavity is when you first open up the animal, and that heat, unless dissipated, can quickly spoil the meat. Since most big game hunting takes place with snow on the ground, one can wash the insides with clean snow to eliminate any blood or other material in the body cavity. Bow hunters and black powder hunters often get their deer in warmer weather and must take extra care to cool the animal off quickly. This also applies to early season moose and elk.

To hang or not to hang, that is a common question. Hanging a carcass in a cool place for a certain period of time tenderizes it. Indeed fine restaurants age beef for up to 35 days before serving. The rule-of-thumb for big game is that the older the animal the longer it must be hung. A week or two is not out of the question for a big buck while, for a young animal, you could almost cut and wrap it the next day. The temperature should be just above freezing, and it's important not to let the carcass freeze solid which stops the aging process. An attached garage is ideal.

Many hunters opt to skin the animal right after shooting it since the hide comes off very easily. However, I prefer to age my deer with the skin on. Keeping the hide on prevents the development of a dried crust on the surface of the meat which occurs if a skinned carcass is aged. Some hunters skin and quarter the animal and then wrap the meat in cheesecloth to prevent drying. This is advisable if you are in a remote location where you must pack out the meat. Hides are heavy!

After cleaning, hanging, and butchering your birds and big game, take care with the freezing process. I double wrap my game; once with clear plastic and secondly with freezer paper. For very choice cuts, I sometimes use a vacuum packer, but the double wrap method works very well. But no matter what you do, label each package, listing the contents and the date it was frozen.

If you follow these simple procedures you will ensure that only wild meat of the highest quality will grace your tables. And you will banish the term "gamey" from your lexicon.

Caroline's favourite: Lynn's Moose Meat Jerky

1 cup soy sauce
2 Tbsp liquid smoke
1 Tbsp Worcestershire sauce
1 Tbsp lite celery salt
1 tsp dry mustard
2 Tbsp cider vinegar
2 tsp black pepper
8 Tbsp brown sugar
2 Tbsp Tenderquick or salt
2 tsp onion powder
2 Tbsp minced garlic (8 cloves)
2 tsp Hungarian paprika
1/2 cup sherry

Slice about 5 pounds of meat less than 1/4 inch thick with the grain, trim all fat (it helps if the meat is partially frozen).

Mix dry ingredients, add wet ingredients, mix well.

Mix meat with marinade and leave at room temperature at least 4 hours or overnight.

Place strips of meat on oven rack, metal screens, commercial dehydrator, etc., and dry at 160°F degrees until dry but not brittle - about 4 hours.

Store jerky in a covered container in a cool dry place.

NOTE: The cider vinegar and sherry may be substituted with 1/2 c Worcestershire sauce. Tenderquick contains nitrates which will help preserve the meat but is not necessary. Regular paprika may be substituted, with the addition of a few shakes of hot sauce.

Bear Sausage

5 feet medium (2" diameter) casings
4 lbs bear meat trimmed of all fat, cubed
1 lb pork fat, cubed
2 1/2 tsp freshly ground black pepper
1 tsp celery seed
1/2 tsp dried thyme leaves
1/2 tsp dried savory
1/2 cup dry red wine

Prepare the casings.

Mix the cubes of meat and fat together with the remaining ingredients.

Grind through the coarse disk.

Grind through the fine disk, stuff into casings, tie off into 3" links and refrigerate to age for two days.

Note: Bear sausages MUST be very well cooked before being consumed

Elk Sausage

5 feet medium (2" diameter) casings
4 lbs elk meat, trimmed and cubed
1 lb beef fat, cubed
2 1/2 tsp salt
2 tsp coarsely ground black pepper
2 tsp cayenne pepper
2 cloves garlic, finely chopped
1 tsp crushed anise seed
1/4 cup dry red wine

Prepare the casings.

Grind the meat and fat together through the coarse disk.

Mix the remaining ingredients together with the meat. Stuff the mixture into the casings and twist off into four inch links. This is a spicy sausage and it is best roasted or grilled.

Bear Stew

When our daughter Marsha was in high school, we were fortunate to have some bear meat. She loved the meat, and her favourite was the bear stew which she would even eat for breakfast. As well, I even decided to render all the fat from the bear which is a slow process of cooking down the fat in cubes in a big roaster in the oven. I managed to make several quarts of fat, which I proceeded to use for pie crusts and making homemade bread which was delicious. A local native fellow heard that I had rendered some fat from the bear and called me to see if I would give him a quart for his elderly mother who remembered baking with it many years ago and would love to have some. And, of course, I was more than happy to give him a jar.

2 Tbsp canola oil
3-4 lbs stewing meat cut in cubes
2 cloves garlic minced
4 onions quartered
2 Tbsp all purpose flour
2 1/2 cups beef stock
1 can stewed tomatoes (19 oz)—undrained
4 carrots cut in chunks
2 celery stocks chopped
4 parsnips cut in chunks
1 tsp Worcestershire

5 potatoes—peeled and quartered
Salt/Pepper to taste

In large dutch oven, heat oil and brown the meat cubes. Add garlic and onions, and cook until softened. Sprinkle the flour over the meat, garlic and onions stirring until browned. Add stock, canned tomatoes, carrots, celery, parsnips and Worcestershire. Bring to a boil. Cover and reduce heat and cook for 1 1/2 hours. Add more stock if stew seems too thick. Add potatoes and cook for an additional 30 minutes or until potatoes are tender. Season with salt and pepper to taste.

Cooking Wild Game Birds

(September 2008)

With some hunting seasons underway and others about to open soon, many Manitobans will be cooking wild game this fall. You may be the spouse or parent of a novice hunter confronted with game for the first time; or you may be a non-hunter who has been given a gift of game meat. Or you are a veteran hunter, but you and your family cook game the same way every time; kind of "stuck in a rut" so to speak. To my family, wild game is simply the best there is. And if you hunt a variety of game, as I do, you get to sample upland game birds, waterfowl, and various big game species. Let's take a look at some simple ways to produce wonderful game meals, focusing on game birds.

Proper preparation is crucial once the bird is in hand. Game birds should be cleaned and cooled as quickly as possible. The cooling process is vital if you want to avoid a "gamey" taste. Gaminess comes about because of improper handling of the animal and is not inherent in the taste of wild game. After cleaning, I always soak my game birds overnight in salted water and rinse them off thoroughly the next day (rinsing is important!) before cooking.

Upland birds

These include the ruffed, sharp-tailed, and spruce grouse plus the little Hungarian partridge. These birds, especially ruffed grouse, are considered by many to be the epitome of wild food. Unless plucked right after killing when the feathers come off easy, most upland birds are skinned leaving a nice chunk of breast meat; white meat for the ruffed grouse and Hungarian partridge and dark meat for the other two. There are hundreds of recipes, but a key to all of them is to not dry the meat out; it's got little enough fat as it is. You can spice up the breast, wrap in foil and then barbecue. Or you can roast it in a very tightly sealed clay baker with a bit of water in the bottom. Putting strips of bacon over them adds flavour and moisture. Or you can just cut the meat into pieces, roll them in spiced flour and then stir fry.

Ducks

Ducks are considered by many to be the most challenging wild game, but a properly cooked duck is almost the best meat there is. You can either pluck the bird and roast it or cut off the breast meat (called "skinning" the duck) and cooking. As with the upland birds keeping the meat moist is crucial, so roasting in a tightly sealed roaster or clay baker (and I mean sealed!) is mandatory. I like to roast my ducks with very high heat (400–500°F) for a short period of time; 20 minutes for small ducks and about 35–40 minutes for larger ones. Take them out soon enough that there is a hint of pink in the meat. And rosemary is a good spice to sprinkle over a duck. Cooking breasted ducks is a bit tricky because they tend to dry out. A Saskatchewan friend last year showed me how to solve that. He sliced the breast meat into thin slices, laid them out on a cookie sheet, doused them with sun-dried tomato dressing and proceeded to bake the lot of them in the oven. Delicious! "Duck poppers" are another favourite in our house. You slice the breasts into thin pieces, roll them up with a little jalapeño pepper inside, wrap bacon around that, skewer with a toothpick and then bake them all on a metal sheet in the oven. You will be shocked at how fast these little appetizers disappear.

Geese

Geese are very abundant, and many hunters have become quite adept at bagging this common waterfowl species. But geese can be challenging, and I know that, in some households, the family has told the hunter, "no more geese!" This is too bad because proper preparation can turn "so-so" geese into a culinary delight. Most hunters breast their geese, and the same recipe for the "duck poppers" above can be used for geese. I'm very partial to goose cooked for many hours in a slow cooker smothered with spices and vegetables with a bunch of sliced potatoes. Also, unlike many hunters, I take the goose legs as well and throw them into the slow cooker. Later in the year I like to pluck some of my fat geese and roast them very slowly in a covered roaster with some water in the bottom. Some folks make an orange sauce for dipping after the roasting process.

This has been just a very quick introduction to game bird cookery, but you should buy a number of good cookbooks. The most comprehensive one is *The L.L. Bean Cookbook* by the company of the same name, but there are many others. And don't forget to search the Internet; there are hundreds of recipes online. But the bottom line is, take care with wild game birds, keep them moist, and cook on the rare side. You'll be glad you did.

Caroline's favourite: Pheasant/Grouse Pie

Serves 10

2 pheasant breasts
2 grouse breasts
(or any combination of the above or by themselves)
1/4 lb mushrooms sliced
2 garlic cloves minced
1/2 cup slivered almonds
2 cups mandarin oranges
1/2 cup to 3/4 cup port wine or sherry
1 can consommé soup
1/2 - 3/4 cup chopped celery
pinch marjoram
salt and pepper to taste

Sauté breasts in 2 Tbsp butter—do not overcook. Remove from pan. Cool and cube.

Sauté mushrooms, celery and garlic in same pan until soft.

Mix all ingredients and pour into a casserole dish.

Cover with pie crust.

Make this 1 day in advance and let the pie sit (uncooked) in the fridge so flavours blend nicely.

Cook just prior to serving at 400°F degrees for 15 to 20 minutes (until crust browns).

Jalapeño Duck Appetizers (A Family Favourite)

Duck Breasts—slice in strips
Bacon
Jalapeños or Hot Banana Peppers

Sprinkle breasts with a little Montreal Steak Spice (optional)

Put hot pepper in middle of duck breast.

Place duck on a piece of bacon the same size.

Roll-up and secure with toothpick.

Broil in oven until bacon is cooked. Duck will be done. Turn over half way through so meat cooks on underside.

NOTE: Try to pick out all the shot from game birds prior to cooking and eating, especially waterfowl which can only be hunted with steel shot. Steel shot is very hard and biting down on a piece of steel shot can easily crack a tooth: I should know. I've done it! Lead shot, which can be used for upland birds, is somewhat more forgiving since it is softer than steel but you should be careful nonetheless. So chew slowly and savour every morsel, and save your teeth as well!

Morel Mushrooms and Fiddlehead Ferns: Two Spring Treats

(PREVIOUSLY UNPUBLISHED)

Spring time in Manitoba is magic time. The honk of the majestic Canada goose fills the air, the frogs are singing their spring chorus, and the "forest elves" have slipped quietly into the woods in search of morel mushrooms and fiddlehead ferns. Of course we're not talking real elves (although many of us do wish they existed) but those dedicated folks who can't wait to get into the woods in search of these two delectable spring delicacies; morel mushrooms and fiddlehead ferns.

Morels are the first mushrooms of spring and are one of the most iconic of mushrooms. Morel hunters abound across much of North America and most wouldn't be caught dead revealing their favourite mushroom spot. Morels have a corrugated cap and a longish stem and are the only spring mushroom. A quick Internet search will show you their exact appearance. And since morels are essentially the only spring mushroom, an aspiring mushroom hunter need not fear any dire consequences.

I find wooded aspen forest pastures to be the best morel habitat. The combination of open woodland and the free cow manure seems to work wonders for morels. But morels are not without their challenges and some years are much better than others. I recall 2005 when morels seemed to be everywhere. My neighbours and I were picking five-gallon pails with regularity and we had more than enough to freeze and dry. But in other years, scarcely a morel can be found, and one is fortunate to pick enough for one meal. There has to be the right combination of spring rain and sunny warm days.

Morels have a wonderful taste and can be prepared in many ways. A favourite method in our neck-of-the-woods is to lightly sauté them in garlic butter and then drench them in sour cream. Pour that mixture over some good rye toast, and you are in seventh heaven. But morels are great in omelets and in any other dish that calls for mushrooms. So when spring next rolls around head for the woods in search of morels.

Fiddleheads are traditionally thought of as an East Coast delicacy and truckloads are shipped across Canada. But what many people do not realize is that the fiddlehead fern, more properly called the ostrich fern, is widespread across the country. And indeed on my own farm we have two large ostrich fern patches. Unlike morels, ostrich ferns are a never-fail spring green. The term "fiddlehead" refers to the young fern which, as they start to uncurl, resemble the curled head of a violin. Ferns grow on the forest floor in moist areas where there is absolutely no wind; quite magical places actually. But you have to be quick since ferns grow exceedingly fast and are soon beyond the picking stage. To me, good picking fiddles heads are two to four inches in length. Each fern puts forth about three to five shoots but I try not to pick all the stems from a plant. And since there are usually many plants in a patch this will not affect the overall harvest. And unlike morels, little searching is required for fiddleheads; once you are in a patch just pick away! But if you are really lucky fiddlehead time and morel time may just coincide. There have been times when we've taken two pails into the woods; one for morels and one for fiddleheads.

In terms of preparing fiddleheads, the rule-of-thumb is that whatever you can do with asparagus, you can do with fiddleheads. Steam them and dab on a pat of butter and you are in seventh heaven. And steamed, cooled fiddleheads are dandy in a salad. Sauté them and place them in an omelet with all the accoutrements and they are "simply to die for." A quick Internet search will find many more recipes.

Fiddleheads and morels are magic spring treasures that will lift you out of the winter doldrums quicker than you can imagine. Who needs to wait for the garden to come on!

Morels

Morels in frying pan

Wild Berries Add a Wonderful Dimension to Rural Life

(PREVIOUSLY UNPUBLISHED)

The aspen parkland is a treasure trove of berries. Each has a specific season, a distinctive taste, and different uses. One of the most common berries is the good old saskatoon which has been a food staple across the prairies for centuries. Pemmican, a mixture of dried saskatoon berries and dried bison meat fuelled Metis buffalo hunters for decades. Protein rich, full of nutrients, and long-lasting, pemmican was nearly the perfect food. Indeed for all the berries we'll be talking about, quick Internet searches will find an endless array of recipes.

In our neck-of-the woods, saskatoons are the first wild berry of the year, and their minute white flowers covering entire hillsides are a mighty welcome sight after a long winter. Saskatoons are a "meaty" berry and somewhat drier than most other berries, and with their sweet taste saskatoons are the most versatile berry of all. Pies, jams, and jellies can all be made with saskatoons with saskatoon pie achieving near legendary status in many communities. In fact saskatoons have been domesticated and "U-Pick" saskatoon farms have sprung up across the prairies.

Saskatoon plants are classified as woody shrubs, sometimes achieving heights of three metres or more. But the productivity of a saskatoon shrub does not really depend on height, and we have had wonderful picking off shrubs that are no more than a metre high. They grow as single berries which makes picking a bit slow. And the saskatoon harvest is definitively variable from year to year in spite of the fact that saskatoon plants are extremely abundant. In some years the saskatoon patches are a sea of blue while in others nary a berry can be found. There has to be the right combination of rain, sunny days, and warm temperatures. I am convinced that saskatoons actually prefer a drier situation, for in wet years there can be millions of flowers but few berries.

The next berry to come "online" in our region are chokecherries. Bitter tasting and with a hard single seed inside chokecherries are the ultimate jelly berry. And don't worry if your jelly fails; chokecherry syrup on pancakes are to die for. Their sour taste, once ameliorated with sugar, creates a distinctive jelly that is a real hit around the breakfast table. Chokecherries grow quite differently than saskatoons. And in a good year you can pick them by the handful; and you kind of "milk" the branch pulling off a multitude of berries with each movement. Filling an ice cream pail takes no time at all.

And lastly we come to everyone's favourite; the high bush cranberry. Known as *kalyna* in Ukrainian, the high bush cranberry has achieved almost mythical status in Ukrainian culture and kalyna jelly is a part of every traditional Ukrainian meal. And with the arrival of the high bush cranberry we are at the end of the berry year. The leaves have turned and the silent, deep woods, the cranberry's preferred habitat, become cathedral-like. There is a debate between high bush cranberry aficionados regarding the best time to pick. Some pick before the first frost and at this time the berries still have an orange tinge and are somewhat hard. They are easy to pick and the "pre-frost" pickers claim that jelly made from the early berries have a better chance of gelling during the jelly making process. We prefer to wait until after the first hard frost. At this stage the berries turn a blood red and are a bit softer. A number will break in your hands so red hands are a clear sign that someone has been high bush cranberry picking. If you get into a good patch it is easy to pick as many pails as you want. What we like about the "post-frost" berries is their pungency. Boiling berries, the first step in making berries, makes the whole house smell like cranberries. More care must be taken with these late berries to make the juice gel so don't be afraid to use a lot of Serto, the gelling agent. And like chokecherries "failed" high bush cranberry jelly makes wonderful syrup.

Wild berries add an immeasurable dimension to country life; they are easy to pick, the experience can be sublime, and the deep satisfaction one gets when gazing on a shelf groaning under the weight of a few dozen jars of jelly is hard to beat. Get out picking! You won't regret it.

Caroline's favourite: High Bush Cranberry Jelly

4 cup of berries
2 cups of water

Squash berries with masher in water and bring to a boil.

Simmer for 3-5 minutes (covered) and then boil rapidly for 10 minutes.

Strain through jelly bag.

Pour into saucepan and add 2/3 cup sugar for every cup of juice.

Stir until dissolved and put on hot element for approximately 8-10 minutes.

Do not stir - boil rapidly - watch it closely.

Pour into hot sterilized pint sealers to 1/4" (.5 cm) of top.

Place sterilized metal lids on jars and screw metal bands on securely.

Process in a boiling water bath for 5 minutes.

If you use pectin, follow directions on pectin package.

Putting Food By

On any winter day, Caroline and I often sit down to a home procured meal of venison from a deer we'd harvested off our land, home grown potatoes, our own pickles, a chutney or two, topped off with two glasses of homemade wine. "Yup," I'd say. "It's another fifty-cent supper, Caroline."

We take a great deal of satisfaction in being as self-sufficient in food as possible. Oh, we're not fanatics about eating locally, so winter California lettuce or an occasional treat of New Zealand lamb finds it's way to our table. Still and all, we take a great deal of comfort when that last bag of September garden potatoes is hoisted into the cold room. And then we happily stare at the year's bounty; a bounty that also includes dill pickles, "dilly" beans, pickled green tomatoes, sweet pickled beets, home made relishes, all manner of squashes, plus wild berry jams and jellies.

In the last few years, we've really taken to canning as opposed to freezing. Even the Old Guide (that's me) put up twenty-three jars of dill pickles on his own one year. Of course Caroline had to "talk me through it" via cell phone (she was away on business) much like that archetypal air traffic controller "talks down" that archetypal passenger-pilot in those archetypal airplane disaster movies! I am happy to say that the pickles made a happy landing!

In addition to growing vegetables for winter use, we take pains to plant those seasonal vegetables that are consumed right out of the garden. We're eating asparagus in May, then baby beets and multiplier onions in June, and by then the Swiss chard is big enough to steam. Soon the first green beans will be appearing to be added to the rapidly growing mix of "steamed garden" that is such a treat in the summer.

Caroline starts to make fresh garden borscht at about this time and the baby potatoes will be here soon. So from May until the fall we eat right out of the garden and make the smooth transition to root vegetables and canned delicacies just in time for hunting season.

A word about cold rooms. If you have an unused corner of your basement, you should think about building a walk-in cold room. Ours is as big as a child's bedroom and features shelves, wine racks and lots of storage area. And many a deer has hung in it. You only need to wall off a corner of your basement, super insulate it, install a door and shelves and voila; you have a cold room to store all manner of stuff. Punch a hole in the plate so outside air comes in but you should be prepared to plug the hole in real cold weather. Potatoes keep in ours from September to May in perfect condition. And it doesn't matter if you live in a city with a limited amount of land to grow a garden. A cold room allows you to buy big quantities of inexpensive vegetables at market gardens and store stuff for the winter. Cold rooms are also great places to "hang" game birds and deer to age them properly. We find that in the dead of winter our cold room stays at between +1 and +5°C, about the temperature of your fridge. So a real bonus is that you have now created a monster second fridge that you will find mighty handy. Build a cold room, store veggies, get canning; you won't regret it.

Caroline's favourite: Beet Pickles

Makes 5 pint (500 ml) jars

8 cups prepared beets (4 lb or 1.8 kg)
3 cups sliced onions (about 3 medium)
2 1/2 cups cider vinegar
2 cups granulated sugar
1 1/2 cups water
1 Tbsp mustard seed
1 tsp each of salt, whole allspice and whole cloves

Trim all but 2 inches off beet stems and cook in boiling water until tender, about 35 minutes. Remove from water and remove skins by easily slipping off beets under cool water. Set aside.

Prepare and sterilize jars and snap lids in boiling water in canner over high heat.

Combine onions, vinegar, sugar, water, mustard seed, salt, allspice, cloves in a large stainless steel or enamel saucepan. Bring to a boil and boil gently for 5 minutes.

Pack beets into a hot jar to within 3/4 inch (2 cm) of top rim. Add boiling liquid to cover beets to within 1/2 inch (1 cm) of top rim. Remove air bubbles by sliding a rubber spatula between glass and food. Wipe jar rim removing any stickiness. Put on snap lid and screw band until fingertip tight. Place jars in canner.

Cover canner returning water to boil. Process for 30 minutes. Remove jars. Cool and check seals. Store in a cool, dark place.

CAROLINE IN COLD ROOM

Caroline with Garden Produce

Wild Spring Foods Create Delightful Meals

(MAY 2003)

Gardening is a popular activity in Manitoba, and we gardeners eagerly await the first fresh vegetables of the year. But there are ways to get a jump on the garden by harvesting edible plants in spring. You will get that first taste of spring without having to work at all! In fact you can create whole meals of spring greens and mushrooms gathered while taking walks through our beautiful countryside.

A case in point was last week when good friend Ted Poyser dropped in for a few days of fishing and some rural R&R. Our first foray was to a nearby lake where we caught some chunky prairie pike. On the way home I suggested to Ted that we get some greens to go along with the fish and he readily agreed.

One of the finest spring foods is the fiddlehead, the new shoots of the fern species known as the ostrich fern. Sold at great cost in Manitoba's gourmet stores, few Manitobans know that wild fiddleheads abound here. Fiddleheads are young ferns, so named because of their curly stalks that look remarkably like the head of a violin. Ferns grow very quickly so fiddlehead time is short, but if you hit it right you can fill up a cooler. Ted and I gathered all we needed from a patch near home. We only took those that were tightly curled and avoided any that were starting to stretch out.

"How about some spinach?" I asked Ted. In answer to his puzzled look I walked to a patch of newly emergent stinging nettles. Now we've all fought this tenacious imported weed in our yards, but the young shoots make a great addition to an omelet or as a companion green to steamed fiddleheads. My fingers tingled as I picked the ends of these prickly plants but that soon went away in anticipation of the meal to come.

To add to our bounty, I had earlier picked some morel mushrooms, the epitome of wild foods. Like beautiful buttery brown ghosts they one day appear on the forest floor in spring. Capricious and mysterious, their abundance changes dramatically from year to year depending on rainfall. Mushroom picking is an important part of Manitoba's heritage, no more so than in Manitoba's Ukrainian community. Known as "smoirzhi" in Ukrainian, mushroom picking is an important rite of spring in my area. While people talk freely about the pails and pails of morels they have picked, don't even bother asking them for picking locations. Such information is jealously guarded and handed down from generation to generation.

Morel habitat is hard to describe. I'd describe it as "open aspen forest with a bit of grass, all on somewhat moist-ish soils." Morel habitat has a certain "feel" to it that you will recognize as your experience grows. Lightly grazed wooded pastures are good places to start.

Back to supper. Now that we had gathered all of the ingredients, it was time to prepare our wild meal. Caroline simply sautéed the mushrooms in butter although on other occasions we've added onions and sour cream to the mix. The fiddleheads and nettles were steamed, and Caroline sprinkled sesame seeds and red wine vinaigrette dressing over the entire mixture. My contribution was to prepare the "blackened" pike, done Cajun-style. "Simply delicious" was how Ted described this meal, made all the more satisfying because we'd done it ourselves. Wild food is the original "fun food."

There are number of good books on wild plant identification. The mushroom hunters bible is *Edible and Poisonous Mushrooms of Canada* by J. Walton Groves, published in 1979 by Agriculture Canada. Morels are one of the few spring mushrooms out there so you are quite safe picking them although you will want to be able to distinguish the edible kind from its inedible and mildly toxic cousin, the false morel. Groves has good photos of both plus many more. For other plants I like Gerald Mulligan's *Common Weeds of Canada* also out of Agriculture Canada (1976) and then there's the somewhat technical A.C. Budd and K.F. Best book, *Wild Plants of the Canadian Prairies* again from Agriculture Canada (1969). Learn your plants, get out the cookbooks, and enjoy!

Preparing Early Season Geese for the Table

(September 2010)

Manitoba waterfowl hunters are in their glory during these gentle September days. The weather is warm, the birds abundant (and a bit naïve, if the truth be known), and there is enough daylight for the "country kids," to rush out to the goose field after school. On this last note, I was recently hunting with a young lad from Onanole, who must go unnamed, who said that his dad sometimes lets him skip school to go hunting. And while I revere education, I most certainly approve of dads who occasionally let their kids "play hooky" to go hunting. You go Dad!

Early season geese have little fat and can be a challenge to cook. Most of the meat by far on a big Canada goose is breast meat and many hunters carve out these parts. The result is two "steak-sized" pieces of meat that are great eating but somewhat dry. But, cooked right, they are simply delicious. My brother, Tim, who is a bit of a gourmand in his own right, and his family simply rave over the following recipe:

Barbequed Stuffed Goose Breasts and Blueberry Sauce:

Marinade

One cup soy sauce
2 Tbsp balsamic vinegar
1-inch piece of ginger, finely chopped
3 garlic cloves minced
7–10 juniper berries, crushed (optional)

Add ingredients, bring to a simmer for 5 minutes. Take off stove and allow to cool before adding the meat. Marinate for a maximum of 2 hours. Marinading in a ziploc bag works well.

Stuffing

1 large onion, sliced thin
1/4 cup of pine nuts
1 cup of sliced mushrooms
2 cloves garlic, smashed
1 tsp of rubbed, sage
1/2 cup of couscous, wild rice or quinoa, cooked
Goose tenders, if you saved them

Caramelize onions, with olive oil. Add salt at the beginning.

When onions are half done, add in mushrooms, garlic and pine nuts. Continue to sauté until the mix is well browned. Add in sage, and your favourite cooked grain towards the end.

Sauté the finely-chopped goose tenders (which should have been marinating with the meat) and add in last.

This stuffing is now ready for stuffing in your marinated goose breast, in which you previously plunge-cut a pocket for the stuffing. BBQ the stuffed breasts at about 400°F to medium-rare, but no more.

Slice in 1/2" to 3/4" widths before serving. Top with the blueberry sauce.

Blueberry Sauce

1 cup meat stock
1/3 cup of finely diced onion
1 cup frozen blueberries (use fresh if you have)
1 cup red wine
2 Tbsp butter
2 Tbsp maple syrup
1 tsp of rubbed, dried sage
Salt, pepper to taste

Add stock, onions and blueberries to a large frying pan and bring to a boil

Add in wine and cook to reduce.

When reduced by half, add in butter and maple syrup. Reduce by half again.

Add in sage, salt, pepper, and simmer for a couple of minutes before serving.

Hint: you know you have reduced this enough when the blueberries really stand out in the sauce and the sauce itself is quite thick. When you take the reduction this far, the flavours are intense. It's worth the wait...."

Wine and Wild Game

(December 2008)

With most hunting seasons just about over, many Manitoba hunters have freezers full of wild game and are looking forward to feasting on Mother Nature's bounty. And for many, the proper wine brings out the very best in wild game. Good wine—and not-so-good wine for that matter—has accompanied many a meal of wild game. And to get some advice on wine selection I turned to Diane Nelson, wine columnist for the *Brandon Sun* and journalism instructor at Assiniboine Community College. Her column, *Vine Lines*, is a regular feature in the *Sun*.

"My husband, Ken McPhail, is an avid hunter," said Nelson, "We usually have all types of wild game in our freezer, and I love them all, but I'm especially partial to caribou and grouse. The beauty of game is that one can enjoy a wide variety of tastes and certain wines bring out the best in each type of game."

Nelson is anything but a "wine snob" and firmly noted that we should all drink the wine that we like and not be bound by somebody else's rules.

"The old wine rules are long gone," she explained. "So don't be afraid to have white wine with red meat and vice versa. There is such a variety to choose from and you can enjoy them all."

Our family had just finished cutting up our last deer, so I was eager to learn about venison wines.

"I'm really partial to the Australian Shiraz's when it comes to deer meat," Nelson said. "Their full-bodied flavour really brings out the best in venison."

WILD GAME MEAL AND WINE

She went on to wax rhapsodic about her very favourite deer recipe which requires wine for cooking.

"I take a deer backstrap and do it medium rare on the barbecue," she explained. "I then take two cans of consommé soup, undiluted, and mix that with an equal amount of wine. Throw in some garlic cloves and reduce it all to one-quarter or one-eighth of the original volume. The result is a salty, beefy brown sauce that is simply delicious when drizzled over the barbecued backstrap. Crack open that Shiraz and you have a meal fit for a king!"

Nelson noted that ducks and geese can be a bit tricky.

"A lot of people prepare duck with orange sauce, which I really like," she said. "And then I'd go with a sweeter Merlot since duck can overpower a white wine. The sweeter Merlot complements the sweet taste of the orange sauce."

When I asked about goose, she was quick to recommend a Chardonnay.

"The smoky and buttery taste of the Chardonnay goes well with wild goose," Nelson explained. "Goose can have intense flavours that the Chardonnay complements. Also, don't hesitate to try a red such as a Pinot Noir.

Ruffed and sharp-tailed grouse, especially sharp-tails, are her very favourite wild game.

"I love the dark red meat of the sharp-tails, and there's nothing like a Pinot Noir to bring those flavours out," she exclaimed. "And for ruffies, I'd want a Chardonnay or a Pinot Grigio."

And as for other game such as elk and caribou, which are milder than venison, she recommends a Cabernet Sauvignon since both species have a more delicate flavour.

I knew we had just scratched the surface of the wonderful world of wine and am already looking forward to more conversations.

The Inestimable Caroline

(PREVIOUSLY UNPUBLISHED)

It has become clear, dear reader, that making it in the woods alone is difficult; not impossible, but difficult. We had the case of Henry David Thoreau who ostensibly went to "live in the woods" but if rumours are true, he spent half his time cadging meals from the local neighbours. A "perfect wife" would have solved that problem.

In my case I *was* living in the woods by myself, and it became clear that I needed a perfect wife, and in 1988 she came along. In this case it was the inestimable Caroline. Let me illustrate the characteristics of said "perfect wife" and how they were determined.

Caroline was living in a city when we met, and after some cajoling (begging actually), she accepted an invitation to come for a weekend visit to my little log cabin in the woods. Now I was clearly smitten, but to be frank and somewhat sexist, not every woman takes to country life. Contrary to popular opinion, it is men who are the romantics; I grew up dreaming of becoming a trapper, fly fishing for trophy salmon, and dog-sledding up North for a caribou hunt. Women, by and large have little time for such foolishness, being rightfully concerned about such mundane things as raising children, paying off the mortgage, and putting food on the table.

But on that first visit, I had to make sure that Caroline actually *liked* country living. It was September, as I recall, and the bull elk were in full rut and bugling like mad. I knew a good spot in Riding Mountain National Park to go and call for elk, so I suggested an evening walk in the Park. Not having experienced the thrill of a bugling bull elk at close range she readily agreed.

It was the perfect evening: calm, clear, and cool. After parking the car and walking north for a kilometre or so we started to hear the spine-tingling call of big bull elk. It was pure magic! We stopped and called and got immediate responses. As we moved up the trail, we heard ahead of us what was obviously an artificial call. We soon caught up with my neighbour Dave and his daughter who were also calling elk. We teamed up with Dave and began calling.

CAROLINE AND MOUNTIE WITH A BRACE OF SHARPTAILS

We were on the edge of a fifty-hectare clearing that had conifer woods on the other side when we heard the most magnificent call from what was obviously a really big bull who was just inside the line of trees. Dave called and the trees parted and out he marched right towards us. By this time I had the bright idea, given the rapidly diminishing daylight, that we could "make like an elk" and walk right up to him. Bright boy! So with Dave calling behind us I bent down, grabbed a startled Caroline by the waist, and said, "Put your arms in the air and start walking!"

She complied and the elk was treated to this strange sight of a four-legged creature, with what looked like antlers, walking towards him in the dim light. Dave kept calling and I swear I saw the elk tilt his head as if to say, "What the ... ?"

But the elk was in full rut and was in no mood to back down from whatever strange creature this was. So he kept on coming. By this time my enthusiasm turned to anxiety as I clearly hadn't thought this whole scheme completely through. But Caroline, the trooper, kept on walking. We got about twenty metres away from this very mad elk when discretion got the better of valour and I said, "Let's get out of here!" I still wonder what this elk thought when he saw his "rival" split in two and run away.

Caroline thought this was great fun and asked to be part of more adventures. *Hmmm*, I thought *She looks like a keeper*. Soon after, we were married and the rest is history. Caroline cans vegetables, cuts up deer, knows which mushrooms to pick, and makes the finest wild berry jelly anywhere. We've had many adventures since that day with the elk: The tale of the frozen muskrat in the microwave; The legend of the flying squirrel behind the toaster; The sorry saga of the duck in the fireplace; and of course, The adventure of the black bear shot out the kitchen window. These have all become great family stories. The inestimable Caroline just smiles through it all and looks forward to the next one

The Gift

(PREVIOUSLY UNPUBLISHED)

The summer of 1971 was one to remember as far as I was concerned. I had just finished my second year of Zoology at the University of Manitoba and had been taken on by the federal Fisheries Service as a summer student on the McKenzie Valley Environmental Study. Environmental Impact Statements were in their infancy, and this particular study was designed to gather baseline fisheries and aquatic information prior to the construction of the McKenzie Valley gas pipeline.

Apart from the seriousness of the subject matter, I was in seventh heaven! Here I was, a little Manitoba boy, in the land of Dene Indians, the gold rush, and Jack London all rolled into one. My job, if you could call it that, would be to travel the McKenzie River, up and down from Fort Simpson, to set and lift gillnets and to "sample" the fish species that we had taken. Was there ever a better job for a romantic prairie boy who simply refused to grow up? Didn't think so. I had some knowledge of boats, fish, and gillnets, having spent the previous summer in Northern Manitoba on another fisheries study. But nothing prepared me for the "Mighty McKenzie." This mighty river, the thirteenth longest in the world, wends its way from Great Slave Lake to the Beaufort Sea. The volumes of water it discharges are staggering, and numerous communities use the river as a highway, a source of fish, and for drinking water. And apart from some large rivers in Russia, the McKenzie River is one of the largest waterbodies in the world to be in largely a pristine condition.

We had hired Dave MacPherson, a Dene First Nations person, to work with us, and soon he and I became inseparable. The boss realized that, with my experience at setting and lifting nets and academic background, and Dave's superb river navigation and guiding skills that we were a team that could deliver comprehensive results. So Dave and I were left to our own devices. We had a map that showed where we had to set nets, which we did. We'd travel "up south" and set nets in the proscribed locations. By the way, local folks there say "up south" since the McKenzie flows North i.e. the southern country is higher than the north; hence "up south" and "down north." The days flowed by; setting and lifting nets and then analyzing the catch before delivering the results back to the base camp. Lunch consisted of fresh fish over an open fire washed down by good McKenzie Valley tea. All in all an idyllic existence. Not to mention that I was getting paid for the entire summer!

But there was one day I'll remember above all others. Dave and I were travelling "up south." I was napping (as usual) in the bow seat while Dave drove the boat. At some point, and for a reason I cannot explain, I sat up and looked ahead. And about three hundred metres in front of us a bald eagle was crossing the river at right angles. *Neat*, I thought. But when the bird was halfway across the river a primary feather detached itself from a wing and wafted down to the water in front of us. The feather spun in the current and Dave, without a word, moved the boat towards it. I plucked the feather from the surface and looked at Dave. We didn't say a word.

This feather has been with me ever since that day in 1971. Has it helped me? Who knows? Look, I am a product of a modern scientific education, a career in science and technology, as well as biological research. I demand proof before I accept anyone's word. Evidence is the gold standard for all my decisions. But why did I keep this feather for all these years? It was with me through graduate school, my careers, my marriage, my political career, and the building of my home in the woods. And it has been only recently that I have looked at the feather with a new appreciation. Is this why I have had such a happy life? Is this why I have managed to overcome adversity in my own bumbling and stumbling way? Is this why my family, children, and grandchildren are healthy, happy, and prosperous? And is this why I will always love the inestimable Caroline? Perhaps. One thing is for sure; the eagle feather will be with me to the end.

A Granddaughter Comes into Our Lives

(Previously Unpublished)

We knew that our daughter-in-law Lainee was expecting, but the three o'clock in the morning call from son Tony (in August 2009) was still a surprise.

"Come to the hospital. Lainee's in labour!"

We packed up real quick and began the three hour drive to Winnipeg. We were worried, to be sure, but confident. Lainee was a healthy Mom-to-be and there had been no complications. And sure enough, when we arrived at the hospital, Lainee and Tony were the proud parents of the most beautiful granddaughter in the world (of course you expected me to say that).

She was named Eden, an apt name if there ever was one. Naturally, given my predilections for the outdoors and country living, her first gift from me was a little camouflage "onesie." What a sap, eh? Nevertheless Caroline, now referred to as "Nana," and I already were making great plans about how this little bundle of joy would become a country girl. By this time, we had decked out the spare room in the log house as Eden's room, and I think that I bought her first fishing rod when she was only five months old. Furthermore, I was bound and determined that her first taste of meat would be wild game. And for her first meat, I chose a piece of ruffed grouse, which I pureed into a liquid. She didn't know what to make of it and spat most of it back, but I know that a little bit managed to make it into her tummy.

"There," I said "she'll like wild game forever."

The subsequent four years, with the strong support of her parents, have been a magical exploration of the natural world and country living with Eden. I am firmly convinced that the affinity we humans have for natural landscapes and country experiences is rooted deep in our DNA. After all, for 99% of human existence we roamed over natural landscapes.

Naturally, being mad gardeners, we introduced Eden to the magic of growing things. And naturally, one of our gardens is "hers" and is named, of course, the "Garden of Eden." The list of her farm experiences is long and growing. She has been on the snowmobile with 'Papa' (that's me), helped pick out the family Christmas tree, dug worms for fishing, help drive the tractor, made snow angels, picked raspberries (or "rabbies" as she called them), and has become quite possessive about "The Farm." In fact, one day she and I were walking on our newly planted wheat field and I said, "This is Nana and Papa's field."

She fixed me with a determined gaze and declared, "It's MY field too."

"Yes it is, little one," I replied smiling.

Fishing with Eden, of course, is a real treat. Not that she can't be cantankerous; like all little ones, she has her moments. But fishing with Nana and Papa is a special joy for all of us. And the fact that she was introduced to rough and tumble country living at an early age means that she has a toughness that belies her few years. She'll sit on my lap as I drive the boat and takes water in the face in stride; in fact she revels in it especially when we are bouncing over rough water. She caught her first fish at three and was fascinated with the pike swimming in the live-well. She was equally enthralled with the fish cleaning afterwards. I have found that little kids are not squeamish in the least and she and I had great fun examining the "innards" of that pike. I pointed out the various parts and she was fascinated when I cut the pike's stomach open and a whole bunch of small fish poured out. That was her first lesson in ecology; big fish eat little fish. And, naturally, she is a born fish eater which completes the circle.

I am convinced that the freedom of country living creates confident kids. Being free and taking measured but safe risks teaches a child that exploration, inquisitiveness, and problem solving have their own rewards. And, of course, a kid like Eden will take it too far. One day last winter Eden, who was three years old at the time, was in the yard with Mountie, our big gentle Chesapeake Bay Retriever. Caroline had to go back into the house for a moment but when she came out; no Eden. Naturally she was frantic but soon found Eden walking North on our farm road with Mountie at her side.

"Where in Heaven's name are you going?" Caroline asked.

Eden replied matter-of-factly that she was walking to Auntie Candy's, our neighbour two kilometres to the North.

"How were you going to get back?" said Caroline.

"Well, Nana," Eden declared with that know-it-all look of a three-year-old. "I'll just follow my footsteps back home!" Smart kid.

Since that time Tony and Lainee have expanded their family with the addition of twins; the boy Senon and the girl Esmee. I'm already dreaming of new little fishing rods, fishing trips, boating, country adventures and introducing two more grandchildren to the joys of the natural world and country living. It simply does not get any better than that.

Eden and "Papa" Fighting a Big Fish

Hunting with Dad

(October 2000)

Father died last week. It was not unexpected, since he'd become progressively weaker after a series of strokes. At age eighty-seven, he was confined to his bed in a veteran's nursing home in Winnipeg. In the great scheme of things, an older person's death is not an especially remarkable event; the funeral is held, condolences are given and life goes on. Still, for the children it marks a passage into a new stage. For the first time in your life, you have no father.

Funeral planning is traditionally done by the offspring, and it was no different in our case. My brother, sister, and I sat around the table, struck by the finality of our loss. As we met, one thought kept recurring; I wanted to speak at Dad's service.

As I thought about my words, I realized that I wanted to talk mostly about hunting with Dad. He was a good man—a kind father, a devoted husband and wonderful grandfather—but I wanted to zero in on those hunting experiences that so affected our lives.

Dad emigrated with his family from Czechoslovakia in the 1920s. They moved into Northern Ontario and became dirt-poor loggers, cutting pulp by hand, hauling it out with horses, and shipping it by rail to nearby mills. It's an old story, but an important one, repeated many times by millions of members of the World War Two generation. This was a generation that Tom Brokaw has called the "Greatest Generation" and with very good reason.

Fast-forwarding to Winnipeg in the 1950s, Dad was now married with two little boys, Tim and I. We loved stories, but all we ever wanted to hear about was Ontario. At bedtime we'd ask Dad to tell us about his life in the Ontario bush. Over and over the poor man had to tell the same stories about how, with his old Eatons single shot .22, he'd shoot grouse and rabbits for the next meal, or pick off big, spawning pike for the first fresh fish of the year and about the unspeakable agony of having to "put down" his faithful dog. For us it was Robert Service, Jack London, the explorers and *courier-du-bois* all rolled into one. To us these hunting stories stirred up an atavism so strong that it was almost palpable. It created an unquenchable thirst to be outdoors, and learn the profound and subtle lessons of nature.

All of these thoughts were cascading through my mind when it was my turn to speak at Dad's funeral. I described Dad's Ontario experiences and related my remembrances of the time when it was our turn to go hunting with Dad.

You know how it is when some images are so strong they almost make you flinch? Such are mine. We'd get up early, but bright-eyed and excited, and Dad would make the hunter's breakfast of eggs, bacon, onions, and rye toast washed down with weak tea. When we at last we broke free of the city limits and drove to our boreal forest cottage east of Winnipeg, it was light and time to hunt.

Our hunts were but one expression of a collective experience since rising from the dawn of humankind. When I now think of our little troop tip-toeing down a woodland trail, I liken it to a little wolf pack with the experienced hunter leading the way and the unruly wolf cubs behind. The autumn forest smells of rotting leaves, pungent fall berries, and balsam fir and the image of Dad, with his horn-rimmed glasses and a brown hunting coat, are burned into my memory. I can bring them back simply by crushing some balsam needles and inhaling.

Over the course of the morning we'd work our way along forest paths until Dad would stop. We stopped too. He'd seen something. We would move up along side peer into the thicket, our hearts pounding. There, rigid and motionless, would be a ruffed grouse. We held our breath as Dad sighted down the old .22 and, when satisfied, he'd pull back the bolt, sight again and fire. Dad only shot for the head and, if his eye was keen, there would be the tell-tale flutter from the forest floor that signified a clean kill. With that, Tim and I would dive into the thicket, grab the bird, and run proudly back to Dad. We'd examine the bird, admire the feathers, check out what it had been eating and then fight to see who would carry it. Smiling, Dad knew that he had to get another, so each could carry a bird. Back home, we'd proudly show our birds to Mom who would ooh and ahh as only a mother can.

As I spoke at the funeral, I could see the older fellows in the congregation nodding their heads as latent memories of their own upbringings or those of their grown children came to the fore. For my brother and I, these experiences led to careers in conservation. Our caring for the land and its inhabitants continues as he fights the good fight in the bureaucracy, and Caroline and I live back in the woods, stewarding our little piece of the Earth.

In the June 20, 2000 issue of the *National Post*, Donna Laframboise writes that where she comes from, "...hunting and fishing are an integral part of a way of life that has been passed down through the generations." She notes the importance of special hunting places "...where rites of passage from adolescence to adulthood occur, where people of modest means and humble dreams commune with nature and nurture their spiritual selves."

For me, therein lies the issue. It is this side of hunting and fishing that is absent from the national debate on firearms, hunting, and our relationship to wildlife. Hunting represents an enduring connection with our honourable past. By hunting and eating what I kill, I reaffirm my connection to the natural world and my place within. To put it another way, you cannot understand the world without eating some of it. Grass, trees, prey, predator, birth and death—the age-old connection must continue if we are to survive as a species.

It is no accident that the greatest of our conservationists were all hunters. Conservation pioneers and hunters like Aldo Leopold, Theodore Roosevelt, Sigurd Olson, Henry David Thoreau, Prince Philip, Albert Hochbaum, Ernest Thompson Seton, and James Audubon, to name a few, all understood his connection and fought to preserve the ecological systems that support wildlife and ultimately all of us. But as the population urbanizes and wildlife experiences are relegated to the Internet, this real and organic connection to life itself is being lost. That is why many of us ardently cling to an ancient past. The world is moving at light speed, morality is whatever you want, and ideas come and go. But to me, hunting is an eternal connection to my family and its history, to my hunting and gathering ancestors and to the land.

As Paul Shepard states in his book *The Tender Carnivore and the Sacred Game*, "His primate forebears and more importantly his million years as a hunter-gatherer are the sources of the meaning of human experience—both past and in the life cycle, from birth to old age, in maleness and femaleness of every individual." Hunting is one of the most joyous experiences that a person can have. It's not just about the killing, nor the chase, nor the eating; it is all of it bound together. José Ortega y Gasset has a chapter in his book; *Meditations on Hunting* entitled "Hunting and Happiness" wherein he talks about the pure joy of the hunter that transcends all other activities. This is what critics of hunting want to take away from me.

Do you recall those old Western movies where the Indians who were killed went to the "Happy Hunting Grounds?" Leaving aside the Hollywood cliché culture, this notion is surely grounded in deep spirituality. After a good life, the hunter would ascend to a place of flowing streams, beautiful forests, and abundant game where for eternity he would, with family and friends, pursue the creatures of his dreams. In time I'll be there, hunting with Dad.

This Has Been a Wonderful Journey

(OCTOBER 2010)

It is with very mixed emotions that I write this, my last column, as Hunting and Outdoors Columnist with the *Winnipeg Free Press*. My bride, the inestimable Caroline, and I are embarking on a new phase of our lives whereby I will be attempting to launch a political career.

But when you move on, you always think about what one leaves behind. And in my case it is this column and you, my faithful readers, who have made it so very worthwhile. My column has been a labour of love and it has been my privilege to showcase to you the "lifestyle of a hunter." As an aside, many of you were no doubt bemused by the decided lack of "how to hunt" pieces, which are typical of many other hunting publications. But I can now let you in on my little secret; I'm actually not that good of a hunter. So suggesting tactics, strategies, and advice on "how to bag that big buck" was simply beyond me!

More importantly, however, I wished to convey the joys of living the life of a responsible hunter who resides in a beautiful part of Manitoba. Whether it is the explosive flush of a ruffed grouse, a big buck in the evening light, or the magic time known as "dawn in a duck blind," a hunter's life is filled with an awe and wonder that words simply cannot describe.

Hunting is a funny thing. Some are puzzled as to why a person would hunt and ultimately kill; and all the while expressing a deep and profound respect for your quarry and the landscapes that sustain our precious wildlife resources. In my case that passion for hunting and fishing, which I learned from my late father, led to a very rewarding career in conservation. It's quite simple, actually. We hunters "take," therefore we must "give back." And we do.

One thing that columnists live for is feedback from readers. My friendly readers were quick to correct my errors, recount stories of their own, suggest column ideas, and enhance my understanding of their own hunting experiences. I am especially grateful for all those non-hunters who consistently read my column simply because of a lively curiosity about what we do "out here." I cherish one letter from an elderly lady who recounted her joyful childhood on the family farm. She ended her letter with, "Keep us posted about the simple joys, Mr. Sopuck."

On another occasion, a father was overcome with emotion when describing his son's first deer. "Because of that experience together," he said, all choked up, "I will have my son forever." I had a lump in my throat over that.

Hunting is one of those timeless activities that gives us respite from an increasingly hectic world and harkens back to a simpler time. But a time that is still very much with us as befits a hunting species that evolved over three million years. And long after the game has been eaten, the stories and memories remain. Or as Henry David Thoreau said:

"I went to the woods because I wished to live deliberately, to front only the essential facts of life, and see if I could not learn what it had to teach, and not, when I came to die, discover that I had not lived."

It has been wonderful to have these years with you all. Thank you.

Afterword

Compiling this book has been a labour of love and, in many, ways can be considered my life's story. From my first fish at age four, to speaking at my father's funeral, to an increasing appreciation of one's own mortality, I have been a creature of the natural world. And in that world there are many treasured friends and I wish to thank them all.

Firstly, I must express my profound thanks to my family, especially the inestimable Caroline, who have taught and nurtured me all these years. My writings would have been simply impossible without the generous contributions of my hunting companions and those who allowed me into their lives as outdoors-people and good country folk. And I simply must tip my hat to those professionals who dedicate their careers to the conservation of our precious fish and wildlife resources.

And lastly, I must express my humble gratitude to those fish and wildlife that have allowed themselves to be pursued by me all these years. To those I have killed and eaten, I thank you for giving yourselves to me and my family so we can be true participants in the natural world. The eating of wild game that you have taken is the sacramental aspect of hunting; it completes the circle. For those fish I released and the wildlife that eluded me I wish you a joyous life in this world and the next. I am truly a fortunate man.

About the Author

Robert Sopuck is a fisheries biologist who has spent decades in nature conducting fisheries research, wildlife surveys, and working on the conservation of our precious fish and wildlife resources. He has farmed, trapped, and guided people on many outdoor adventures. He was the Outdoors Columnist with the Winnipeg Free Press and penned over 250 columns on wildlife, country living, hunting, and natural history. Robert is a passionate advocate for the countryside and for those people who live in it. To Robert, the phrase "living off the land" is no mere slogan but a profound description of how he and Caroline live their lives. The message herein is that there are ways of living that touch the Earth lightly while providing deep and profound answers to some of our most vexing questions.

Robert Sopuck is also a Member of Parliament in the House of Commons.

Printed in Canada